What
N<u>ow</u>?
Navigating the
Twenty-Something Years

Metro Associates, Inc.
3501 Arkansas
St. Louis, MO 63118
314-772-8993
www.Fruitful-Life.net

Printed in the United States of America

ISBN  0-9722625-0-4

# Contents

## Chapters

# Dedication

To Jesus Christ, the savior of my soul and my entire life.
In precious, priceless memory of Genorah Stewart (Granny)
and Mark I. Green (my brother)

# Acknowledgments

## To my family:

To my wife - My girl Carol, God sent you and you changed my world. He sent me a hidden pearl. I love you. To my sons Christopher Michael, Jonathan Mark and David Matthew: You are my beloved sons in whom I am well pleased. To my father and mother James and Jane Green who paved the way. To my brothers & sisters (Pastors Raphael and Brenda Green, Elder Jonathan and Cynthia Green, Pamela Keys and Lillian Stewart, Mark Green, who is with the Lord, and Desiree Green). There was a time when I wanted to get away from the Green name. Now I prefer no other because of you. I send a smile to heaven for Granny Stewart and my brother Irwin who I never got to know. To all my nephews and nieces, all my cousins, aunts and uncles especially Aunt Jerline Green (We were never just your brother's kids), and to three of my adoptive spiritual children, Carlette Mack, Tiffany McCreight, and Calvin Banks who gave me my initial baptism in appreciating and understanding teens and twenty something young adults. I don't have the space to name all my spiritual sons and daughters, but you know I love each and every one of you.

## The Metro warriors:

who touched our life, marriage and ministry through the years: Theodore and Cassandra Boldin, John and Charlene Burris, Rodney and Jean Cutler, George and Kim Rose, Jerrod and Treniece Jones, Robert and Shawn Parrish, Shelby and Renee Johnson, Frank and Robin King, Wayne and Sheila Clarke, Chris and Veeta Jackson, Byron and Patrice Reddick, Gladys Morris, Jerline Tuggle, Carrie Head, Barbara DeClue, Rochelle DeClue, Joshua Generation, MY

People, N.O.C., Infantry, the "20 Something" Crew, the Remnant Catcher team, the GIFTS ministry, our Metro family hour, MCWC musicians and praise teams, Generations & Praise, every couple we were privileged to teach in our Pre-Marital class, all the elders, deacons, departmental and outreach leaders of MCWC, administrative assistants, Rhonda Jones and Kristie Jursch, and the entire staff of MCWC. To Barrick and Debra Fields and the multi-media ministry. To Pat Gregory, Kim Tolliver, and the proofreading team. I love y'all! Finally, much thanks to my editor, Angel McKay (You kept my feet on the ground) and her husband James who unselfishly shared her with us.

## The prophetic voices that spoke into our lives:

Gene Bacon, Melissa Clayton, Dr. Mark Chironna, Elder Yul Crawford, Dr. Jerry Horner, Pastor David Ireland, Bishop Flynn and Carolyn Johnson, and Lattie McDonough. We are living out every word and prayer since you laid your hands upon us.

## My partners in the faith:

Mark and Dawn Lawrence, Dave and Angie Burrows, Glenn and Michelle Forde, Manoah and Toye Collins, Aaron and Gretchen Layton, Dr. Dale and Carla Conaway, David and Bonnie Johnson, Matt and Mary Harris and Dr. Corrine Conway.

No one does anything in this world on his own. This book bears the signature and mark of every single one of you in some way or another. It could not have been done without you in my life.

# Foreword

Rare are the times in this life when we have the opportunity to be under the influence and instruction of wise and innovative masters of their trade. Rarer still are the individuals who are not primarily driven by unhealthy desires to be successful in their trade, but are purely motivated to help others acquire and experience the highest quality of personal and relational fulfillment possible rather than achieving mere worldly success. Such is the case with the author of this brilliant work written by my brother and colleague, Christopher Green.

The highest form of living is to do so in a genuine committed relationship with God and to love others through the incomparable power, exquisite love and quintessential wisdom that is available only through the Lord Jesus Christ. The so-called wisdom of the various ages and gurus of eras both ancient and contemporary will never topple or transcend the concepts and practical advice Chris gives us in this book. "Pastor Chris", as those in his home church affectionately call him in urban St Louis, is irrefutably qualified to present the principles he sets forth in this book. The call of God along with his integrity and proven track record unquestionably certifies his mandate and right to address this issue. This he does with astounding accuracy, keen insight, reliable recommendations and dependable direction. At the time of this book's release he serves as senior associate pastor where he has been a covenant member and team leader since 1987. My wife, Brenda and I, along with countless others have been enlightened, enhanced and elevated beyond measure as a result of his investment in our lives. The spirit of loyalty, camaraderie, unity, servant-leadership, sacrificial obedience and steadfast love in which he operates has positively affected us all and there is much fruit that remains to the glory of God because of Carol's (his precious bride of over twenty years) and his labor. For several reasons I am pleased to be among the first to recommend this book. It is biblically sound and perfectly timed. Although he is specifically addressing those of you in your twenties, the principles presented are relevant to everyone irrespective of age, generation, gender, ethnicity, religious affiliation, nationality or culture. They are therefore workable in every place. This is one of the outstanding features of this book. If the Lord blesses it to gain a large international readership, it could perhaps prove to be a powerfully positive generational link as well.

Finally, I am persuaded it is a book that will be used of God to produce inestimable blessing in your life. The principles set forth in this book are straight from God's word and heart. They cannot fail. Neither will you if you heed them.

On a more personal note, I am pleased to say that a man that I have known all of his life presents them. I am his oldest brother. Also, as his pastor, I, along with our wives and other leaders, have had the pleasure of watching and assisting him in his personal spiritual development and we have had the privilege of serving together in ministry for over twenty years. We have learned much together. It is an honor to commend him and his work to you, for they are one in the same.

This is the type of book you will want to pass on to those in future generations. In so doing, the redemptive purpose and untapped potential for every human being and nation on the planet can be fully realized. I only wish I had this book when I was in my early twenties. If you have ever said or heard someone say, "If I had only known then what I know now" – stop and realize that this moment is the "then" that you longed to have previously. This book is a treasure chest of practical insight and direction that will definitely help you. Even if you are out of your twenties, you can be helped or assist someone else in their twenties through giving them the wisdom in this work.

As you read it, you will be challenged, changed and elevated to a new level between you and God, within yourself and with others. Most importantly if you heed the insights and directions given, you will discover and fulfill your destiny just as God intended. So will those with whom you are related. May God minister to you as you prayerfully read it and may he cause Chris, Carol, this work and you to be all that is in accord with His providential purpose.

Let's help him get this message to as many people as possible...especially those living and working in the urban world.

For Christ's Glory Alone,

Raphael Green
Senior Minister/Founder
Metro Christian Worship Center
CEO/President
Metro Associated, Inc.

Metro Christian Worship Center is a budding congregation worshipping and serving in urban St Louis. Metro Associates, Inc. is an innovative and multi-faceted church and community development ministry headquartered in the St Louis region also. Both the local church and Para-church ministry are committed to the fulfillment of the great commission concentrating their labor in the urban world.

# Preface

At the time of the writing of this book, my wife, Carol, and I oversee the teens, singles, and pre-marital preparation ministries in our church. Throughout the years of urban and inner city ministry, we have observed most young people struggling through the twenty something season of life the same way we faltered and floundered through it. There was transition right after high school and college. We faced difficult transitions through career changes and definitely transition into marriage. Later there was the transition of leaving our twenties and moving into our thirties. There is something about the transition of the twenty something years that will mark you for life. We have the scars to show it. Out of our ministry to teens, young adults, engaged or married couples, and life experience has come this book.

-Christopher G. Green

# Introduction

## Cancel the high-school class reunion plans

I was 27 years old with a wife, a son, and a mountain of bills. I had been in pursuit of the American dream and the pursuit had become a disaster. It was the summer of 1987 and my father was helping me move out of our three- bedroom home, which featured a full finished basement and a big back yard. My wife, Carol, and I were facing foreclosure and as a last chance show of leniency, our mortgage company gave us a deadline to move out of the house so they could transfer the property to someone else. We moved into a two-bedroom townhouse apartment. To add insult to injury, this move was on the same weekend I had planned to attend my high school class reunion.

We later discovered since someone was already lined up to assume our loan, an official foreclosure would not show on our credit report. We would have to live with a "voluntarily surrendered property" rating on our record, which meant a credit rating of eight out of a possible lowest rating of nine. It was like falling from a 30-foot cliff from 15 feet instead of the full 30. Thank God we did not die from the fall. One year later, still unable to maintain our monthly obligations, we moved into my parents' house. They graciously opened up their home to my small family. I was filled with frustration as I tugged and pulled our refrigerator into position for my father to help me unload it from the truck I had rented. The deposit to reserve the vehicle was made with our last $200.00. My life was like that refrigerator, unyielding and cold.

Rewind the tape about ten years. After graduating from high school in 1977, I moved on to college. Like many other excited freshman, I was in awe at Oral Roberts University. There I met other starry-eyed teenagers of 18 or 19 years. We did not know what was in store for us. We had no idea that this simple decision to obey the voice and direction of God, was leading us into intense internal turmoil and fierce spiritual opposition. We did not know the price of obedience, and we were not mentally fortified for the process needed beyond textbooks and exams. Many of us did not heed the warnings of the guest speakers in the chapel services or the advice of our professors. The idealism of the teenage years wore thin quickly and the only thing left was whatever seeds of truth that had truly taken root in the tender soil of our youthful lives. Suddenly we were faced with life long decisions about securing loans, choosing classes, declaring majors, and establishing friends. At the same time we were trying to avoid detours and distractions. For some of us we faced death, disappointments, and disillusionment for the first time.

Disillusionment was a word my parents used, but the meaning had been foreign. In my first three semesters of college disillusionment became real and I could not handle it. Angry with God and on the verge of backsliding, I quit school and set out to handle life on my own.

### It's you and me against the world!

I met my future wife, Carol, at the university, but we were separated from each other after our first year of college. She returned to her home, Harrisburg, Pennsylvania with no foreseeable way to come back to O.R.U. She had run out of money. I was living and working in Tulsa, Oklahoma. It was more fuel added to the angry furnace within me. Carol and I set out on a course to be together and our philosophy was taken from this phrase, "It's you and me against the world!" We worked jobs, saved money, and she made her way back to Tulsa. By the summer of 1979, we were back together. Our timing was terrible, but we were meant to be. I knew this was true because God spared our lives in the midst of my foolishness. In March of 1980, we survived a drunk driver crashing into us. Our car was turned upside down. God used the accident to turn our lives right side up. We made plans for me to go back to college so at least one of us would be academically prepared. I was back in school in the fall of 1980, but I received a phone call from a collection agency demanding payment on my student loan even though I was re-enrolled. I snapped and quit school in a silent rage against God. I asked, "Why won't You help me, Man?" I felt if He wanted me in school I would not have to fight for it, especially in a faith-based institution. Three months later (December 1980), I married Carol.

## Real life stomped on our plans

Now fast forward to June of 1987 where the plans to take Carol to my high school class reunion were demolished. I planned to show everyone how successful I had become. I was going to display my beautiful wife like a trophy. I was going to brag about our home in the suburbs, two cars, and a new baby boy. I was going to show them how life had been going for Christopher Green. Yeah, right! It did not turn out that way. Let me take you through the series of transitions that led to that day.

After leaving college and getting married, we moved to St. Louis. It was the start of a season of getting somewhat back on track with the will of God. We worked hard and found a small apartment as we settled into daily life. In February of 1983 we began traveling and ministering evangelistically with my brother, Raphael Green. We sacrificed our personal plans to help him build and fortify the ministry, Love Reach, Inc. I believe God called us to do it, but it was partly a way to escape the tedium of everyday life. Five month later we returned to St. Louis after my brother married and moved to Virginia. We were in limbo. We started looking for jobs and a place to live. One of my best friends asked us to move back to Tulsa, but we eventually settled into God's direction for our lives, which meant living with my parents until we found jobs. Boy did we find jobs! Finally we got paid! **But we compromised the purpose of God for salaries and benefits.** We set out to fulfill the American dream.

For three years things were seemingly successful until real life stomped on our plans. We progressed from renting an apartment to buying a house. We bought two cars. I was excited when Carol revealed she was expecting our first child. Life was good, but I was trying to prove my worth in spite of my failures. We joined a good church, but I was so buried in my new career in financial services that I sporadically gave time and money to the ministry. Sometimes I was very diligent and faithful. Most times I was working toward fulfilling my own dream. I had taken up where I left off when I quit school, still trying to make it on my own.

Carol's employment ended six weeks after our son was born. Her position was "phased out" while she was on maternity leave. **MY INCOME, ALONE, COULD NOT SUSTAIN US!** We did not have college degrees or favor with God so better paying jobs was not an option! After about six months, we tried to sell the house. As previously mentioned, on the day of my class reunion we had to release the house and return to apartment life. A few months later, money was still so tight we surrendered the good car. The day came when we had to move back into my parents' home. I came to grips with living according to my own will and the terribly selfish theme "It's you and me against the world."

We had to start all over again because I was like the brother of the prodigal son. He never left home physically, but was far from home in his heart. In my heart I was a long way from the will of God. We began to build again by humbling ourselves. We had to return to right fellowship and submission to God, my family and the church. It was not until these things were in order that our lives turned around.

The summer of 1987 was the most pivotal period of our lives because it was our transition into purpose and destiny. It was the summer Raphael and Brenda Green started the church (Metro Christian Worship Center). It seemed like terrible timing for us, but God saw it as perfect timing for Him. Pastor Raphael asked us to help them at a time when we did not feel we could help ourselves.

## The twenty something years are a time of contradiction

Now fast-forward to the present. God has blessed us tremendously. Since 1992 we have been ordained as associate pastors, serving with one of the most innovative preachers, teachers, and urban ministry pioneers in the Body of Christ. Through the years we shared our story and the lessons learned from the twenty something season in life. Out of the ashes have come precious nuggets of wisdom **(N.O.W.)**. These nuggets are for young adults single or married, in church or un-churched. Maybe others (30 something and 40 something) will also benefit because this inspirational insight is for anyone who is in any stormy season that can be described as "transition."

The transitional twenty something years are a time of great contradiction. You feel like a little kid in a big adult world; where you get no respect, but lots of bills. You have big dreams, but awaken to nightmares. Contradictions, man! This is especially true for the generation born during the 1970's and 1980's. They have suffered the fall out of the self-centered attitudes promoted during those years. Today this generation desires family and reality, but they don't know how to get it. They need solid answers because their next decision could be their last. Everywhere they turn, it is life and death. Dating is Russian roulette. Corporate employment is a gamble at best. So, whom can they trust? They are living with contradictions!

I am not going to answer all your questions, but I will attempt to place principles into your hands **to** help you get to the answers. It is easy to get lost in a maze of clever clichés so I will not bore you with fancy phrases and unrealistic solutions. I just want you to avoid dead ends. Unashamedly, I will refer to the Bible as a basic reference for life. It is the most enduring book in the history of mankind and in spite of numerous attempts to snuff out its existence, the truth of the Bible has positively impacted every person, family, nation and generation that has embraced it. I will also refer you to other authors and leaders who have a track record in helping people. My desire is to connect you with the source and resources you need for this phase of life.

The issues I am targeting are not unique to one specific generation. The questions you are dealing with are the same questions your grandparents and parents faced. They are the same questions your children, nieces or nephews will face. Every generation will deal with this transition. As society changes, wisdom should be passed on to the next generation to enable them to find their way through this season.

I personally believe, in many ways, my generation did not pass on the tools for dealing with the twenty something years. For the most part, the boomer generation (born 1944 -1964) rebelled throughout their twenty something season. They made decisions with little regard for the future. Now their children have grown up without the benefits of Godly or practical wisdom. This depravity is being expressed in a generational wave of frustration. My intent is not to criticize the boomers, give excuses for the next generation (the busters) or roll out the red carpet for the bridgers behind them. I wrote this book to help you navigate through **your** "twenty something" season successfully. **It was written to help you in the time of life when many of you are** stumbling between where you used to be and where you want to be.

# Chapter

# I

# Nuggets
# of
# Wisdom

# Chapter 1

"The American Reality: You realize that you needed four or more years to graduate from college. You realize paying $137.50 a month for rent and utilities was not bad at all. You begin to wonder how you survived earning $3000 a year on college work-study programs now that you are earning $30,000 in corporate America and just barely making it. You realize you need the favor of God over your life and the indwelling of the Holy Spirit to survive the cares of this life and the deceitfulness of riches. In your early twenties, you begin to realize that those who are in the 'Look what I have obtained' mentality really do not have a sense of peace. You realize knowing your purpose becomes more necessary because you have to know who you are in Him and not the standards of the American Dream. The only way it is going to be truly obtained is to have your priorities in order. 'Seek ye first the kingdom of God and His righteousness, and all these things shall be added.' That is 'The Father's Dream' and it is the dream we should strive to fulfill."

- Anonymous e-mail on the Remnant Catcher
(Young Adult)Network

**Everyone wakes up from the dream world.**

Have you ever had the most wonderful experience imaginable and awakened to discover it was just a dream? How crushing! You were not a millionaire, living in a mansion, married and playing with your kids. It was Tuesday morning. You jump up and rush out of an empty apartment to get to a job that you hate. That is what it was like for many coming into the twenty something season. Like the buzzing of an alarm clock, life woke you up abruptly from the world of dreams. Everyone has experienced the wake up call.

I find it amazing that no matter what path one has walked, what level of education one achieves or what kind of family up bringing one had, everybody still comes to a place in their life where they are asking, "Is this all?"

My wife, Carol, and I have listened to and advised scores of young people who have graduated from high school, college, or obtained a G.E.D. (certification in American secondary school academic proficiency for individuals who terminated their formal schooling process). They seemed to share the same mental and emotional states. They find themselves depressed because of the mundane routines of life, hostile attitudes of co-workers and bleeding in the traps of credit cards and personal loans. College graduates are stunned when they are forced to take minimum wage jobs. The outlook on life appeared to be the same for everybody.

We also discovered young adults agonizing over the same **issues**. Matters involving conflict, confrontation, disappointments, unforgiveness, anger or pride seemed to throw many young adults into great confusion about the purpose for their lives. The constant nagging complaint and question was "What next? What now?" We saw the frustration of possessing a big dream with very few practical steps or connections to fulfill it. Something never connected in the teenage years on how to make it through the twenty something years.

Just like we had experienced, some were in limbo due to the dismantling of the unrealistic points of view they held about life. When they tried to live out their beliefs, they found in the REAL world, their personal worldview did not come into focus. No matter what, the factors of clashing personalities, money shortages, and limited time spoiled the outcome of their expectations. Even if one had a job in their field of training, the managers and supervisors they worked with did not stick to the rules they had been told in college to honor. Some have asked us, "Why did I bother to go to college and spend all that money just to get a job to work with people who behave the same way we did back in high school?

We find many young adults missing or even rejecting the answers and ways God has provided to take them through the twenty something years because they feel:

     1.) no one understands them

     2.) inadequately prepared for this season

     3.) God and life are unfair

     4.) it is too hard to figure out what God is saying and doing

     5.) there isn't any practical advice available to be successful in life.

I realize there are plenty of crooked things you could be doing to make it in spite of these challenges. You might lie, cheat and steal with the best of them to be successful, but we won't go there!

We know it is frustrating to see the outcome (whether positive or negative) of family and friends, without fully understanding how they got their results, so, let's look at the issues that cause you to miss God's solutions to your biggest problems.

**"Nobody understands how I feel!"**

After church services one Sunday morning a young lady who heard about this book approached us. When we told her the subject matter she made gestures to suggest it would not relate to her life. We began to tell her how the various chapters in the book addressed a young adult's transitions into future plans, but once again she insisted it had nothing to do with her. She proceeded to tell us five of her friends had gone into the homosexual lifestyle and she wanted to move away from home and never come back. Realizing she had not made the connection between the book and what she was going through, we said to her, "The book is about: relationships, pressures and the time of life you are in".

A couple of days later Carol talked to me about the incident. She expressed to me, "This has been a common response when we have talked to the twenty something young adult in particular. Unless we name or express exactly, verbatim what they are going through they don't relate to the Godly principle or word of wisdom that will settle any personal situation they are in. 'That is not my issue' is a common response." She went on to say, "I believe the response is one of pride. Before they are able to see how much we really understand where they are coming from, it seems we must have the same circumstances in our own life to convince them of the need to apply what we are relating to their situation. This attitude says no one has ever been through this. No one understands how I feel."

God has a way of purging this attitude in transition. You may not have met someone who has been through exactly what you are going through, but there are many around you who have walked this path before. Just think of the teenagers who are watching your life. If you try to tell them you understand how they feel because you have gone through it too, they look at you as if to say, "You still do not know how I feel because my experience is different than yours." You know what I mean. They give you the same facial expressions you gave people when you were a teenager. Now you understand what those twenty year olds were trying to tell you. Now see yourself in the learning position again. Now the older folks, like me, are trying to say that even if our experiences are not identical, we still know how it feels to be in your twenties. We know how it feels to be excited, hopeful, unsure, intimidated, lonely, unemployed or stuck in a dead end job. **EACH GENERATION HAS A WORD OF COUNSEL FOR THE NEXT. IF ONLY THE NEXT GENERATION WOULD LISTEN.**

### Why didn't you tell me that life was like this?

For many years when I heard the Bible story of the prodigal son, I never realized it was as much about the elder son who stayed home, as it was the son who left. I also believe it describes a season in life everyone goes through. Some go through it in the teen years. Most seem to meet it after high school. Just to make sure we are on the same page, we will look at the story first hand:

Then He said: "A certain man had two sons. And the younger of them said to his father, 'Father, give me the portion of goods that falls to me.' So he divided to them his livelihood. And not many days after, the younger son gathered all together, journeyed to a far country, and there wasted his possessions with prodigal living. But when he had spent all, there arose a severe famine in that land, and he began to be in want. Then he went and joined himself to a citizen of that country, and he sent him into his fields to feed swine. And he would gladly have filled his stomach with the pods that the swine ate, and no one gave him anything. **But when he came to himself,** he said, 'How many of my father's hired servants have bread enough and to spare, and I perish with hunger! 'I will arise and go to my father, and will say to him, 'Father, I have sinned against heaven and before you, and I am no longer worthy to be called your son. Make me like one of your hired servants.' And he arose and came to his father. But when he was still a great way off, his father saw him and had compassion, and ran and fell on his neck and kissed him. And the son said to him, 'Father, I have sinned against heaven and in your sight, and am no longer worthy to be called your son.' But the father said to his servants, 'Bring out the best robe and put it on him, and put a ring on his hand and sandals on his feet. 'And bring the fatted calf here and kill it, and let us eat and be merry; 'for this my son was dead and is alive again; he was lost and is found.' And they began to be merry. Now his older son was in the field. And as he came and drew near to the house, he heard music and dancing. So he called one of the servants and asked what these things meant. And he said to him, 'Your brother has come, and because he has received him safe and sound, your father has killed the fatted calf.' But he was angry and would not go in. Therefore his father came out and pleaded with him. **So he answered and said to his father, 'Lo, these many years I have been serving you; I never transgressed your commandment at any time; and yet you never gave me a young goat, that I might make merry with my friends.** But as soon as this son of yours came, who has devoured your livelihood with harlots, you killed the fatted calf for him.' And he said to him, 'Son, you are always with me, **and all that I have is yours**. It was right that we should make merry and be glad, for your brother was dead and is alive again, and was lost and is found." (Luke 15: 11-32) (1)


This is not a scientific study. I have a few statistics and polls, but what I am saying to you is based upon my personal experience and the people, young and old, that we have ministered to since accepting our true calling in 1992. We have watched young people progress through life. We have walked with many of them through some awfully trying moments. As each one has searched out their path, we noticed a disturbing trend in their transition from our teen ministry into college, the military, or the workforce. They seemed to drift away from us (which is a normal phase), but they rarely returned. Oh yes, they would come home for the holidays, but many were distant, just as I had been. After a period of secular indoctrination, freedom from parental control, and self indulgence in some, not so secret vices, the looks on many faces asked, "Why didn't you tell me life was like this?" For some there was a bit of anger and resentment behind the smiles. For others there was a cynical smirk I felt was due to the belief their pastors and parents were stranded in the past. They, on the other hand, had been enlightened to vast and new possibilities for their future. Most were simply caught somewhere in between. The responses to this new awakening phase in life, concerned us.

## The strategy became clear in a time of prayer

We needed answers to our youth and young adult dilemma so we started attending youth conferences in 1996 beginning with Youth Alive in Nassau, Bahamas. The conference host was a casual acquaintance from my brief days in college, Pastor Dave Burrows. We crossed paths again in a youth conference in Norfolk, Virginia in 1997 hosted by a very close brother and sister in Christ, Mark and Dawn Lawrence. During the conference in Norfolk, Pastor Dave asked me to speak at the 1998 Youth Alive Conference. This was quite a surprise because we there looking for answers, not opportunities to speak. Just before the conference Carol and I attended a Teen Mania Acquire the Fire Youth Leaders dinner. I had never met the founder and president of Teen Mania, Ron Luce, but an O.R.U. friend invited us. It was a set up by God. We were impacted by the statistics revealing over 80% of the teenagers in America's churches leave the church after high school and rarely, if ever, return. I was alarmed by this information because we had seen this disturbing pattern in our church, too. We responded by getting our teens involved in the Acquire the Fire conference and by recruiting teen ministries with whom we had personal relationship. Carol and I went to Youth Alive with a fire and zeal to turn this trend around.

A year later, I distinctly felt we should attend the 1999 Youth Alive Conference, even though I was not on the roster to speak. I felt God had some answers for us. I always feel like I am a student and there is something more to learn. We made a deliberate effort to be in the workshop hosted by Pastor Mark Lawrence.

He talked about different ways to maintain a connection with your college-aged students. I came away from the conference with a new focus. When we returned home to St. Louis, I began to pray about God's plan for us to connect with the post high school young adults.

The strategy came very clearly in a time of prayer. God gave an idea to meet with the young adults in an informal setting in the fellowship hall of our church. My first concern was that it would be perceived negatively as a singles only meeting. In America, for some churches, a singles meeting can almost be the same as a secular nightclub. So the Lord gave us the strategy to shatter this perception. The ministry was open to all young adults, single or married. We did not focus on dating issues, but on all relational matters. We talked about things common to ALL young adults. Negative stigmas and views were eliminated immediately. Single mothers sat beside married mothers without embarrassment or shame, because they were there to talk about life growing up in the 1980's and how it affected them today. The first thing I noticed was young men attending regularly and in far greater numbers than I had expected. The single young men sat next to the married young men and the mysterious singles vibe was driven out of the atmosphere. The male presence made the young adult ministry legitimate. They did not feel like they were being brought out and put on display for young ladies to view, review, and pick or discard.

We started the College and Career Young Adult Ministry of Metro Christian Worship Center in September 1999. Our focus was on Getting the Father's Heart. It was a monthly Friday night meeting, and we made time for our church leaders to share their life experiences during their transitional twenties. We had some very special moments in those early meetings. There were spontaneous songs of worship and frank discussions about personal hurts and memories. It was a welcome outreach. As the reputation of the ministry grew, the young adults began to return. It was not just a physical return. It was a return of the heart. This eventually led to the establishment of a thriving ministry for single adults, G.I.F.T.S. (God's Internally Fortified and Tested Singles) which was divided up according to seasons of life: 20's, 30's, 40's, 50's and so on. This ministry has helped many identify and appreciate where they are and make the changes necessary for the next stage of life without regrets, remorse, or anxiety. We spent our first nine months with the young adults focusing on the story that Jesus told about the father and his two sons and on Proverbs 1, which lists some very specific aspects of life where the wisdom of God needs to be applied in order for one to face and overcome obstacles.

One of our young adult ministry daughters wrote a song, which captured the essence of the early days of that ministry:

The Eldest Son
So many times you tried to talk to me.
I didn't answer.
In prayer didn't seek your face.
I often wondered why you seemed so far from me.
I wondered why it seemed you weren't there.

In the Father's house I lived.
Not really knowing His will.
I didn't know I was a trophy of His grace.
I had never really seen His face.

My life has been showered by your mercy.
I have salvation by faith through grace.
I often wonder how You could love me so.
Why on the cross you chose to wear all my guilt and shame.

Now in the Father's house I live.
Understanding His perfect will.
Living through the gift of His grace

That the world would know of His fame.
Written by Angel P. McKay Copyright 1999

We shared in those first nine months what we will share with you in this book.

## So what is a twenty something young adult supposed to do?

In this age of information breakthrough, I believe what you need in the twenty something season is wisdom. Here is the reason I say this. What do you do with all the information that has been made available to you? Then what do you do about all you do not know? For many of you the basic seed sown in you has been this: You survive and thrive based upon education and information. The problem comes when you take only your education and information into a world where the rules are changed at random by authorities. They use your education against you and hold back information from you. Many of you have discovered, in this world, what you do not know can kill you, and the level of education you have allows people to identify and manipulate you. Racism and sexism demonstrate two ways how information is used against you. So what is a transitional twenty something young adult supposed to do?

Some of you have tried to escape this dilemma by moving to another city, trying a new job, or changing your college major. Some of you have even made a career out of college because you are afraid to make the next step (Face life's challenges outside of the classroom). Many of you are just trying to pay rent and utilities, provide food, and maintain a healthy social life. Family, friends, churches, clubs, and employers seem to always ask for more of your time. It seems they assume you have extra time and energy because of your singleness or youthfulness, but the truth of the matter is you are so mentally worn that on weekends you feel like sleeping from Friday night until Monday morning. But the clothes have to be washed and more bills have to be paid. You have things you **should** be doing that you **don't do.** The things you **shouldn't** be doing, that's what you **get done** faithfully every weekend or whenever you have a day off.

Just like the elder son in our Bible reference, you have spent a lot of time working in the field and you are tired of seeing your wasteful brothers and sisters get away with murder. Many of you have friends and family who seem to be progressing quite well even though they seem to do far less work. There are reasons, good and bad, why this is happening. They have excelled in the world while you continue to work in the Father's field with no apparent reward or thanks. This has led to much frustration and anger directed not only at them, but also now toward God Himself. How unfair it feels to work and plan only to wake up to the celebrations of others while you are taken for granted. Listen to me! Many of those who seem to be moving far ahead of you will come to themselves too.

### You need answers right now.

What we have discovered and have been passing on to people in the transitional twenty something season is what we laid as a foundation for our own life. You need Godly wisdom. There is something in God's heart that He longs to give to you. He never intended for you to feel like you were handed a road map with nothing to identify where you are and where you are going. So right here, right now, I pray that you would settle down and receive from God all He longs to give to you. You may feel you need some money RIGHT NOW. You may feel you need a job RIGHT NOW. You might be saying, "I need to be married RIGHT NOW." Many of you have physical, emotional, and mental stress and you say, "I need a break. I need some relief RIGHT NOW." So stop and surrender unashamedly to God and ask Him, "What am I supposed to do with my life?" Prepare yourself for His answer.

"You need My wisdom RIGHT NOW. You need a NOW

**35**

word. Only My NOW can answer your questions. Only My counsel can give you the NOW connection from your past, through the present, into your future."

## "All that I have is yours."

The thing you are supposed to do with your life right now is to receive the heart of God, your Father. Many of you have been like me. I was living in the Father's house without understanding the Father's heart. I was working in the Father's field, without ever partaking of the fruit of the labor. Remember the father's answer to his angry elder son: "Son, you are always with me, **and all that I have is yours**." * Can you receive this promise from God? He says, "All that I have is yours." The added blessing in the statement is that it has **always been yours**. You do not have to look around and compare your progress to anyone else. There is a specific plan just for you. Though you may have heard this before, you need some practical steps to find your path and purpose. Together, we will walk through the discovery process.

## A Treasure Hunt

To discover your path and purpose there are some things you have to understand about God's way. Proverbs 25:2 says, It is the glory of God to conceal a thing: but the honor of kings is to search out a matter. *

God has declared you to be a king and it is the honor of kings to **search out** the thing God has concealed. No, God is not playing a game of hide and seek. He wants to give you greater insight into His ways. Psalm 103:7 says, He made known his ways unto Moses, his acts unto the children of Israel. *

From this scripture we can see there is a difference between God's ways and His acts. Moses had a higher level of relationship with God than the people He was leading. You may be familiar with the acts of God or the many things **He has done for you**. Now He has brought you into a season where **He wants you to understand His ways or the reasons why He does what He does.**

He is requiring that you put away the immature understanding of life, which says, "God must do What, When, and How I say because He is supposed to supply all my need." This is a very childish understanding of God. You must remember when you talk to God, that **He is God**. He holds the universe together. Billions upon billions of miles of space are like an inch to Him. The power of an atomic explosion is like a whisper to Him. Billions of voices and lives are going forth on Earth simultaneously, and He is fully aware of each one of them. He knows how each decision a person makes impacts tens, hundreds, and thousands of other people of whom they may never be aware. So when you consider how and what you say to Him, the first approach is with humility and thanksgiving. It is with submission, awe and respect. It is with love for Him and not out of selfishness. He has taken great delight in concealing His mysteries and giving His children clues. He watches them like a father on Christmas day, with great wonder, unwrap them. Your life is like a specially wrapped gift. He wants you to unwrap the mystery. These gifts are not hidden **from** you, but **for** you. He calls it honorable for **you** to be willing to unwrap the gifts. It is honorable for Him to be able to give you a map to search out the spot where a chest full of diamonds, rubies, and gold are hidden away for you. By going through the searching process, we appreciate the gift and the Giver so much more.

## God's heart is a Father's heart

One of my spiritual daughters dubbed me with the name,

37

Nugget of Wisdom, partly because of the methods God has given me to minister to this generation. As a special Father's Day gift, I was given a hard hat for construction workers with the letters N.O.W. (Nugget of Wisdom), written on it. The sentiment was so very personal and I appreciated the thought behind the gift. Our spiritual children said God used me to come into their lives, like a construction worker, to break up negative things in the foundation of their lives. I would like to take it a step further than just the acknowledgement of the gift in me by referring to the gift God wants to reveal in you. I believe He wants to come into each of your lives like a hard hat wearing construction worker, to break up all kinds of walls and barriers that have kept you from seeing Him for who He really is. He is a Father. The poor images of earthly fathers have greatly distorted the true picture of God.

Carol wept for days when this revelation dawned upon her. Her father left home when she was twelve years old. For years afterwards, she lived with a haunting fear of abandonment and no real expectations for God to do any of the things He promised in the Bible. Things **could** be done, but she did not believe they **would** be done. God distinguished Himself from the disappointment of her natural father. Today, she is a real woman of faith. She sees God as her father. As long as she knows she is walking in His will and plans, she is assured her prayers are heard and answered because His word promises, For the LORD God is a sun and shield; The LORD will give grace and glory; No good thing will He withhold from those who walk uprightly. (Psalm 84:11) *

There are times I jokingly ask her to pray instead of me, because God seems to answer her prayers quickly since she is so full of faith now. This has even led to reconciliation with her natural father. She is my biggest encourager to this very moment. We know how important it is for you to have this kind of breakthrough in your life so prepare your heart to receive from God!

## Nothing is more practical than getting wisdom from God

Sometimes I have been perceived as being super spiritual and impractical with my teaching and advice. I admit this may sound like I am talking about something that has nothing to do with what you are going through, but read the next few chapters. There is nothing more practical than getting wisdom from God.

The success of my life and every genuine leader in yours has come in some way or another by gathering nuggets of wisdom. When I looked at people I admired and wanted to emulate, I always had one question: "How did they get started?" Maybe you have the same question. Someone reading this has a BIG vision. You have written down plans and made proposals, but you do not know where to begin. Professionals can counsel you. Pastors can advise you. Friends can encourage you. However, only God can get you started. It does not begin with an administrative planning meeting or brainstorming. It does not begin with a financial plan, wealthy investors, private grants or church donations. The starting point is right here, RIGHT NOW! Receive the NOW (Nuggets Of Wisdom) word from God's heart to you!

## Nuggets for Navigating

The next few chapters we will uncover eight nuggets of wisdom for navigating through the life transition you are in. It does not matter whether the transition is from college graduation into a career, from single life to married life, from being the child to becoming a friend to your parents, or from being an employee to owning a business; you need these nuggets of wisdom. If you are moving from one city to another, one career to another, or from one church/ ministry to another, you need these nuggets of wisdom. If you are going through a promotion or a demotion, having your first child, or facing the death of a family member, you need these nuggets of wisdom. Change is constant, yet it is so difficult we often make our biggest mistakes while going through it. We will make a snap decision and suffer life long consequences because we cannot seem to navigate the turbulence. How many times have you heard yourself say, "If I knew then what I know NOW..." I am declaring there is a NOW you can experientially know before you make another step. When tragedy hits or success breaks out, you can make sure steps with these NUGGETS OF WISDOM for:

1.) RESOURCES

2.) RELATIONSHIPS

3.) READINESS

4.) REVELATION

5.) RIDDLES

6.) REVERENCE

7.) RESULTS

8.) REPAIRS

# Chapter
# 2

# Resources
## *I Need A Job,*
## *A Car,*
## *and A Bed*

## Chapter 2

The book of Proverbs begins with,

"The proverbs of Solomon the son of David, king of Israel: **to know** wisdom and instruction, **to perceive** the words of understanding." (Proverbs 1:1-2)*

In my own words, Solomon was saying, "The essence of what you are about to read is for you to know wisdom and instruction far beyond a collection of words and phrases. If you get this, you will be able to really hear what God is saying."

When you read the Proverbs you can be so mesmerized by the sayings it is hard to understand them. That is how many spiritual truths are. They are fascinating to our ears, but they don't seem to get down into our hearts. Something seems to disconnect. However, this introduction, in Proverbs, is already giving you a key to unlock the door to a new world for you. It is not only saying that wisdom exist; but it can be known. To know means to recognize, to regard or to experience. (2) Solomon is indicating right from the beginning, you can recognize when wisdom is coming your way. If you are able to recognize wisdom, it is only because you have personally placed a high value on it. You can experience wisdom first hand. You can participate in its process and rewards.

This verse also says there are words of understanding and you will perceive them. To perceive means, to see, observe, get acquainted with, gain understanding, examine, look after, choose, discover. (3)

The importance of this promise is: in the midst of so many voices, opinions, and experiences, you will still be able to see and observe what God's will is for you in any situation. You will not have to be led by polls, popular fads, or persuasive political beliefs. You will be able to discern the word of God and walk in mature understanding.

Right now you may be asking, "Is this practical?". Look around; you can see the results of lives without knowing or perceiving wisdom from God.

The starting point for the transitional twenty something young adults is not the pursuit of a job, a career, or money. The goal for those who feel called of God (if you cannot find your job, career or money) is not the pursuit of a ministry. The starting point is the pursuit of God and His resources for your life.

### "You don't always need money, but you always need God!"

One of the first realities we all faced was the necessity to financially support ourselves which sounded pretty simple until you discovered just how many hours you had to work to make enough to meet the demands of rent or car payments on a monthly basis. Then you had to pay the insurance premiums and buy fuel to keep that car running. Some of you took those credit card offers and discovered just how high a 22.99% annual percentage rate really is. For those who borrowed your way through college or a technical school, you now have the loan payments for what seems like an eternity. As if that was not overwhelming enough, the utilities, electric and natural gas (for some regions of the planet), has left barely enough for food. This leads you to one conclusion: The top priority of life is to earn money. You fell right in step with the drum cadence that sets the pace for the whole world. After all, I think most people believe money (not love) makes the world go round.

For many years as the assistant pastor in our local church, I led the congregation in what we called the offertory worship. It was at this time the tithes and offerings were received for the church. We received the offering only once per week. For several years I encouraged the congregation with Bible scriptures, stories, and testimonials on the importance of the offering. I became well known for this phrase, "You don't need money. All you need is God!" Now before you drop this book and move on to a magazine or TV show that is more in touch with reality, please give me just a few more sentences.

The basis of the statement came from the Bible and personal experience. In recalling how Carol and I recovered from losing everything, part of our submitting to God meant coming in line with the ways of God. Like everyone else, I prayed asking God to supply the money to pay bills and restore our life. His only response was from the Bible.

"Therefore do not worry, saying, 'What shall we eat?' or 'What shall we drink?' or 'What shall we wear?' For after all these things the Gentiles seek. For your heavenly Father knows that you need all these things. But seek first the kingdom of God and His righteousness, and all these things shall be added to you". (Matthew 6:31-33)*.

## You and I don't tell God what to do. He tells us.

As a kid growing up in church I heard Matthew 6:33 all the time. One day I was faced with the choice to live by this Biblical principle or continue to live by the madness of society. To put the scripture in words I could understand, God was telling me to stop trying to earn a living by pursuing money. If I kept chasing money, I would never get my needs met. If I started pursuing God, the resources I need would chase after and find me. This meant submitting to the plan of God in being faithful in returning of tithes (10% of my gross income) and giving offerings to the local church. Then I had to become more responsible in managing my finances. All of these changes simply meant we were beginning to know the **ways** of God. We began to get things accomplished even if we did not have all the money we needed. We would come across special sales. Car repairs were less frequent. Food would last longer. People would give us clothes for our baby. Instead of asking for money, our prayer changed to asking God for what we needed. He began to meet our needs without necessarily using money. In our journey to recovery we moved from my parents' home into an apartment **without praying for money**. We moved from the apartment into a larger apartment **without praying for money**. We moved from the large apartment into a house **without praying for money**. In each of these moves, because of our credit situation, the problem was not only money, but **we needed** someone to give us a chance. Our credit rating was so terrible at the time; our greatest need was for FAVOR, not money. I believe when we choose to only ask God for money, we are telling Him the way **we think** is the best way to meet our need. What if He does not want to use money to meet the need? What if He wants to use something or someone else? Many times we want God to use money so we don't have to be transparent and receive help or advice from others. Submitting to God's way of meeting the needs means being willing to humble ourselves and accepting whatever way He chooses to get the job done. This often means having to expose some of our weaknesses. The Bible shows how God feels when we try to tell Him what to do or what we think about His way of doing things.

"Then the LORD answered Job out of the whirlwind, and said: "Who is this who darkens counsel by words without knowledge? Now prepare yourself like a man; I will question you, and you shall answer Me. "Where were you when I laid the foundations of the earth? Tell me, if you have understanding". (Job 38:1-3)*.
**You and I don't tell God what to do. He tells us.** I believe when

we only ask God for money to meet our needs, we are violating His **way**. I am trying to be very careful to not give the impression you have to get everything right in your life before He will bless you. That leads to a harmful works-righteousness mentality, meaning, you can earn favor, grace and even your salvation from God through good works. This is not what I am saying because the Bible says,

"For by grace you have been saved through faith, and that not of yourselves; it is the gift of God, **not** of works, lest anyone should boast." (Ephesians 2: 8-9)*

However, I am saying when you get to know God's way and begin to live your life flowing with Him, the results are automatic. You know you are going to get wet if you jump into a pool of water. You do not have to guess or wonder. Favor goes with walking in God's ways like wet goes with water.

### God does not answer to money. Money answers to God.

Here is another way to look at it. In the Bible, Jesus Christ said: "No one can serve two masters; for either he will hate the one and love the other, or else he will be loyal to the one and despise the other. You cannot serve God and mammon." (Matthew 6:24)*

As you well know, mammon (riches or money) confronts you and says, "You need me for your rent and food! You need me for everything! Bow to me! Work extra hours! All that prayer and church attendance does not pay bills, but you have to work that job to get your needs met! I am more important than anything else! Do whatever it takes, because you must answer to me!" Then we fall on our knees and pray to God, "Mammon says I need money for my rent and food, so Lord give me the money. " Do you get the picture? We are trying to get God to submit to the demands of mammon. We know we cannot serve mammon so we take it to God and try to get Him to do it. God does not answer to money. Money answers and submits to God. This happens when we turn away from the commands of mammon and say, "Money, I don't need you to make it! I need God." When we faithfully return the tithe and give offerings to the local church, we put ourselves in a position where we have to trust and depend on God.

Some of you have said that you cannot afford to give your money this way. In reality you cannot afford to withhold it. You must release what belongs to God. That is when He commands mammon to release the finances being withheld from you. It does not matter whether it is the Red Sea or the walls of Jericho, nothing can stand in the way of a person who is walking in the ways of God!

## Your greatest resource in the world is God

Why is it so difficult to believe all you need is God since God has all you need? He has provided ways for you to access Him. This nugget of wisdom to be gained is that God is the greatest resource of all. To put it in more practical terms, rearrange your priorities and make God and His wisdom the object of your pursuits. "Wisdom is the principal thing; therefore, get wisdom. And in all your getting, get understanding." (Proverbs 4:7)*

Did you get it! Your greatest resource in the world is God. One of the foundational expectations God has, is that we get His instruction in our life. It is not an option or an elective in a school curriculum.

I see a need to teach people how to practically apply what they have amassed in head knowledge. Sometimes we graduate students from high school and college who will make great professionals but they lack the skills to get along with people, handle money, discern good or bad deals, manage tough times, deal with secrets or recognize the voice and will of God for their lives. They may never run out of ideas, but their hearts constantly run on empty.

Read one chapter of Proverbs each day to practically apply this principle. In doing this you will cover the entire book in a month. Ask God to open up your heart and mind to what you are reading. Ask Him to give you real life experiences to help you get the point of what you have read. You will be surprised as Proverbs opens up before your eyes in every aspect of your life.

The next few chapters, we will uncover the wisdom of God in other areas of importance to you RIGHT NOW.

Chapter

3

# Relationships
*Debts and Debtors*

# Chapter 3

To receive the instruction of wisdom, justice, judgment, and equity; (Proverbs 1:3)*

## My family and friends are changing

Most have assumed when we start talking about the transitional twenty something season in relationships, we are trying to help you find your spouse. Sometimes it seems this subject alone has caused single adults to stay away from church social events. Although some are looking for a spouse, the majorities are trying to discover who they are and what they are supposed to be doing. When marriage is constantly presented to them as a major goal of all their efforts, most are offended. With so many break ups and bad marriages all around them, it is crazy to try to convince anyone that finding a spouse will solve all problems. (I can't go there. We will talk about this in another book.)

Over the years we have observed the difficult issue of changing relationships. No matter how you grew up, everyone goes through big changes with parents, siblings, and friends. People you thought you knew very well seem to change overnight. They may come out the closet with preferences and lifestyles you never knew was a part of their thinking. Some of your family or friends may get married to people you would never have expected them to. Others are practicing co-habitation (shacking), the homosexual lifestyle, or heterosexual promiscuity. Some who were quiet are becoming more outspoken and violent. Others who were daring and bold are now reserved and withdrawn. Even your relationships with your church or religious leaders have changed because they seem challenging and unsympathetic. People are changing and you must recognize you are changing, too.

## Trying to understand another human being

I found it very interesting the next realm of instruction in Proverbs introduces three powerful words: Justice, Judgment and Equity. These words involve conflict, confrontation, scrutiny, and decisions. Ultimately they define relationships. Undoubtedly, the single most important issue for this time of your life, other than resources, is the area of relationships. What is more frustrating than trying to understand another human being? It can be down right discouraging attempting to understand an individual from a different background, ethnicity, Biblical or religious upbringing, or the opposite sex. If you are going to learn how to navigate through and build healthy relationships, these are three words you will have to embrace.

## Justice

According to Nelson's Illustrated Bible Dictionary: Justice is the practice of what is right or just. It specifies what is right, not only according to a law, but also what makes for right relationships as well as harmony and peace. It goes on to say, The Bible speaks more about doing justice than simply the legal emphasis of the English term. Doing justice is to maintain what is right or to set things right. Justice is done when honorable relationships are maintained.

How willing are you to do justice? To understand justice we have the very difficult task of moving beyond the selfish motivations built up in our hearts during our adolescent years. Now is the time where you have to become willing to accept the covenantal relationships you were born into and to do what is necessary to maintain them in an honorable way. Yes, you have to apply justice with your own family. If you already have a good relationship with your parent(s) or your siblings, make deliberate efforts to maintain them. It is so easy at this point in your life to neglect them and move on in your own pursuits.

An occasional phone call, greeting card, or e-mail goes a long way just to maintain a good thing. As we get older we tend to grow apart. Obviously I am not saying you should be personally involved in everything your family does on a daily basis (receiving a nightly report like the evening news on television). I come from a relatively close family, but as we grew up and moved out of our parents' house, we gave each other time and space to establish our own identities. However, there were a few times we would call or write just to let each other know we were still on the planet. Holidays were very meaningful and we would get together for other special occasions (birthdays or anniversaries). The demands of parenthood and the ministry cut into our times together. That is why it is important to do justice whenever you are going through changes in close relationships. It does not get easier as the years increase. One day you will either be grateful for the time you made for your family or you will regret that you did not. This especially applies to those of you raising a family. Do not neglect your children as you try to improve your standard of living. Do not lie to yourself by saying your children will be okay. There are many who must work outside the home, and I fully understand that. For those of you who do not have to and it is simply a matter of waiting until your children reach school age to work outside the home, please do right by your kids. Don't let the day care raise your child. Do justice for them.

## Justice in a broken family

I can hear some of you saying, "Chris, you don't know my family! I don't have that kind of family closeness." Believe me when I say I am painfully aware of the breakdown of families in today's world. Just about every matter that tears a family apart, I have walked through with my own sisters and brothers as well as the young adults we minister to in our local church. The basic question is this; "How do I do justice in a broken family?" The answer is to set things right. I did not say to make things perfect. To set something right does not mean you will establish some fairy tale ending for your family. To set means to posture or position yourself. The first part of setting things right is to face what is in your own heart regarding every person in your family. Where there has been emotional, verbal, physical or sexual abuse, I strongly recommend professional and pastoral counseling. Setting things right must begin in your own heart before you try to say or do anything with your family. I will address this even more in chapter nine Repairs. For now, please take these first steps in setting things right before you attempt any confrontation or communication in a broken family.

1.) Pray and ask for God's grace to face the past.

2.) Forgive and release each offense against you.

3.) Forgive and release each person, not just what they did or said.

4.) Pray for the family member(s) that hurt and offended you.

5.) Confess this to someone you trust and make yourself accountable.

After some inner healing you should be carefully guided through the next process of setting things right. In all fairness, I cannot tell you what to do because there are so many unique situations. There is no "one size fits all" answer. My main point here is that in order for you to navigate through this part of your life, you have to be willing to do justice. Justice is not just a simple matter of deciding what is best for you alone. It is being willing to do and express what is honorable and right in any relationship to repair or maintain it.

## You will always have to be willing to do justice

Obviously, this principle applies in all your relationships. I began with your family because this is often the most difficult place in which to show justice. What is happening in your family is crucial because you are being prepared to face the same issues in your career, community, marriage, children, and in your church. You will always have to be willing to do justice. If you are not willing you will carry unforgiveness and bitterness into all your relationships. Trust me on this one. You will always be sensitive to what is not being done for you. You will become isolated and full of self-pity. You will live with emotional walls surrounding you, always trying not to get hurt. Even if your personality is outgoing and friendly, you will be guarded and suspicious. To avoid being this kind of person, you must not wait for justice to come to you, but become willing to do justice first.

## Judgment

Judgment primarily denotes "a separating," then a decision, it is discerning and separating between good and evil. (5) One of the most misquoted and misunderstood scriptures in the Bible is Matthew 7:1. For years I have heard people say, "The Bible says judge not, so you don't have the right to judge me!" Let's review the scripture. It actually reads, "Judge not, that you be not judged." (Matthew 7:1)*

I cannot tell you how many times I have heard this scripture used by people who are not familiar with the Bible, God or anything religious. They use it to defend their vices, habits, and rebellion. This gross misinterpretation has led to an entire society that believes no one has the right to "judge" anything they say or do. This scripture does not mean this at all according to 1Corinthians 2:15a "...he who is spiritual judges all things." *

First you have to understand the definition of judging to understand the scripture. Judging does not mean making a snap decision or condemning an action based upon personal likes or dislikes. Judging involves evaluating, appraising, reviewing, and

59

then making a decision. It also involves doing all these things based upon a certain standard, code or law. Judgment is something you do all the time. You make a judgment every time you sit in a chair. You evaluate its ability to sustain your weight. You make a judgment before you change lanes while driving. You evaluate distances of other cars. You make judgments when a teacher is instructing you. You made a judgment to read this book and about everything you have read so far. You will continue to judge everything to follow. You will evaluate, appraise, and make decisions about every concept and idea presented to you. The issue is, what are the criteria for your evaluations and decisions. Whether using the laws of physics, logic or the street, everybody judges all the time.

## The Bible does not say do not judge

When you meet people, you make judgments. You just have to be careful how you judge. That is why you have to read more than Matthew 7:1. You must read the verses that follow: "For with what judgment you judge, you will be judged; and **with the measure you use**, it will be measured back to you." (Matthew 7:2) *

The key is to ask, what is <u>the measure</u>, the standard or the criteria I will use to make a judgment. Once you read further than Matthew 7:1, you get the full picture. <u>The Bible is not saying do not judge</u>. It is saying, check out what standard and criteria you are using in your judging. Whatever standard you use on someone else will be the same standard used on you. Now when it comes to relationships, what criteria do you use to evaluate if a person should be in your life? To what level of intimacy will you allow them to be involved in your life? When you meet a person for the first time, what determines if you like them or not? Is it their ethnicity, good looks, tone of voice or eye color? When you come to a decision before you get to know a person it is called making a pre-judgment or prejudice. Prejudice is based on stereotypes and personal experiences. You do not give the person a chance to prove or disprove your final verdict. Your criteria, in these cases, are based upon standards other than God's word.

## God is not afraid of your questions. Are you afraid of His answers?

In the relationships you are presently in, how do you determine how to progress through them? With so many relationships changing in your life, how do you decide how to handle them? Which do you keep and which ones do you let go? Part of the meaning of judgment is to separate good from evil. There are some relationships that must be terminated because the standard of God's word (the measure) dictates there must be a separation. The person is not necessarily evil, but some of the things they like to participate in are evil for your relationship. They are moving in a different direction than you so a decision must be made. For those who are married there are many factors you must work through so please see the suggested resources from Dr. Clarence Walker Ministries on how to handle conflict in marriage.

Judgment is very important for those of you who are in college determining what clubs or groups you should join or what friends you can have. This is especially difficult since we all have a strong desire for acceptance and affirmation. This is a skill that takes time to develop so proceed wisely and cautiously as you explore the world of new friends and faces. You will be confronted with a wide variety of standards and criteria so decide if you are going to live by the standards of God and His word.

By now, you have discovered many things you were taught was truth were merely personal opinions, fears and prejudice. I caution you; do not throw the Bible out the window along with those opinions. In your quest to discover what is true or what is

**61**

a lie, do not throw away your Bible. Take the time to compare everything that you encounter with the Bible in judging what is best. I believe that you will find that the Bible can meet the challenge of every belief, philosophy and opinion. God is not trying to avoid your questions or scrutiny. The real deal is this: Can you meet the challenge when He answers your questions? Ultimately, in your judging, you are going to make a decision about God and your relationship with Him. You should present all your reasoning and questions to Him. You see God is not afraid of your questions. Are you afraid of His answers? He has some pretty interesting answers for you. Did you know that His judgment of you has some verdicts that are totally in your favor? Every judgment is not a negative decree. Many judgments are awesome, like when a decision is made to award someone millions of dollars. God has made some judgments over your life that are priceless, like family, business, career, ministry, honor, wealth, and long life. When you accept His judgments and His standards for yourself and your relationships, it places you directly on the path to fulfill His plans for your life.

## Equity

Carol and I made preparations to get a lot of work done on our house. From the roof to the basement there was a lot of damage. We set out to refinance the mortgage and use the equity in the house to obtain the funds to make repairs. Here's how equity works. We obtained the services of an appraisal company. A gentleman came to our home and performed a very thorough inspection of every single room and corner. He inspected the roof, the walls, the basement and the foundation. Later he acquired information on the value of other homes in the neighborhood. Finally he sent us a long report giving us the value of our home. His report was sent to the financial institution we were working with. Based upon the value of the home, in spite of all the damage, and subtracting how much we still owed on the home, there was still enough equity to obtain the funds to make the repairs. Equity is the value you still have after the damage and debt. Here's a specific example. Let us say an appraiser looks at a home and in spite of all the damage says it is worth $150,000. Even if you still owed $100,000 on your home loan you have $50,000 in equity. This is how much money is available to use to repair the damage. It would look like this:

**Step 1**

| Value of house | $200,000 |
|---|---|
| Damage | -50,000 |
| Appraised Value | $150,000 |

**Step 2**

| Appraised Value | $150,000 |
|---|---|
| Debt | - $100,000 |
| Equity in house | $ 50,000 |

When the Bible says we need instruction in wisdom, for equity it means you still have to be able to see the value in people. When there is damage to your relationship, no matter how much you are owed you have to see greater value. Can you be an appraiser who makes a thorough inspection (Judgment) and see the value in a person in spite of damage? Can you compare other relationships and still see value in this one? Can you posture yourself to make things right and repair the damage (Justice)?

I like the concept of equity because it works directly with judgment and justice. Equity is the goal of the judgment. You are trying to find the value over and above the damage and debt. Equity is the funds available to do justice. It reveals our willingness to do justice and answers the question: Is it worth it to try?

## More damage than value

Sometimes there can be more damage than the apparent value

can overcome. Sometimes an appraisal will indicate there is more debt than value. No matter how you feel about the relationship or the time you have invested, the debt is so high the appraisal cannot overturn it. In these cases, it takes something greater to heal the relationship. Think of the equity as permission, emotional release, time or energy.

The only thing that can release equity for justice is to cancel the debt.

You must forgive. When you forgive, you give the guilty party permission, emotional release, or time and space to begin to make repairs in your relationship. You cannot heal the relationship in any other way. Did you know one of the definitions of the word forgive is to cancel the debt? That is why an apology (doing justice) must be accepted. Afterwards, the equity or funds can be released to repair (do justice for) the damage. An apology does not repair the damage. An apology opens the door to cancel the debt.

Let's look at the damage. Most of the time the damage is more than hurt feelings. It is damage to one's trust. Most times the damage, combined with the debt, exceed the relationship's ability to sustain it. Forgiveness does not immediately restore the trust, but with the debt canceled, it releases enough equity for justice to begin to repair the damage. If you look at it like a financial situation it looks like this:

**Scenario #1**

| | |
|---|---|
| Our relationship value | $100,000 |
| Damage | -50,000 (injured trust) |
| Debt | -50,000 (an apology) |
| | |
| Justice availability | $ -0.00  (No equity. Cannot go on) |

**Scenario #2** - If the debt is canceled:
Our relationship value        $100,000
Damage                        -50,000 (injured trust)
Debt Canceled                    -0.00 (apology received
                                       and accepted)

Justice availability    $50,000 (Equity. Let's make repairs)

**Accepting the apology does not repair the damage**, but again, it does leave us enough equity to obtain what we need to begin making repairs on the damaged trust. It will take some time to heal the relationship and restore the trust. The canceled debt releases the time and space to do justice, to make things right. You can be set in the position or the posture to do what is right and honorable for the relationship.

Most people never move past the first scenario. They want the repairs made before the debt is canceled. They want the equity available by forcing the other person to prove it will never happen again. This actually causes things to get worse. There is no way the guilty person can ever get out of this kind of debt. The debt connected to damaged trust and a broken heart has caused thousands of relationships to fall apart. The wounded one wants the damage repaired, while the perpetrator needs equity. Oddly enough, only the wounded one can make things work again. Once the debt is canceled, equity is released. Once equity is released repairs can be made. Once repairs are made, the value of the relationship will actually increase just like the value of a home increases after repairs and improvements are made. If damage occurs again, and it most certainly will, there is more value and equity available.

I realize these examples are over simplified and my equity analogy can break down at certain points. Many of you have been hurt and disappointed by people repeatedly, yet it does not take away from the simple principle I am attempting to communicate. For those who are in abusive situations and violent homes, I am not advocating staying to be damaged to the point of death. I have personally helped people get out of these kinds of situations so I understand. However, even after walking women and men through these matters, even if the relationship is never restored back to its original status of marriage or best friends, each person still had to come to accept this principle of equity. Without it, you will not move on in life. You will live constantly keeping tabs of how much people owe you. You will wonder why people do not like being around you or near you. It will be because they can sense you have no equity in your equations for life. You will make people feel like they owe you something.

## You cannot repair the damage without funds

Many years ago my former college roommate and I had a very serious disagreement. It was during a season of limbo after Pastor Raphael and Brenda got married. Carol and I returned to St. Louis after several months of traveling evangelistically and my friend invited us to Tulsa for a visit. He offered to give me his car. What I misinterpreted was he was willing to give it to me if Carol and I moved back to Tulsa. While on our weeklong visit, he and his wife took a trip. They left us in their apartment to seriously consider moving back to Tulsa. We looked for jobs for a couple of days, but I just could not shake the word of God over my life. I was supposed to be in St. Louis to help my family work in ministry. One night, we packed our things, took the car, and drove to St. Louis. My friend felt betrayed and used by me. He was expecting us to be watching their apartment and looking for jobs. I failed to communicate my conviction to be in St. Louis. I did not understand the car was not mine unless we stayed in Tulsa. He felt like I had just taken it and broken our agreement. I gave him the car back and for almost ten years we did not speak to each other. We were both hurt. I missed him terribly, but I did not know where to begin to try to repair the damage. I owed him and he owed me. Then one day, out of nowhere he called me. We made small talk until I asked how his father was doing. He broke into sobs over the phone. He told me his father had passed away. He was calling me behind the most difficult time of his life. Out of his pain, he was calling me to cancel the debt. There I sat, the minister, and it was my friend who was making the first move. Immediately, there was equity. We talked about the misunderstanding. We talked about his dad. I poured out my life journey to him because he was really angry with the Lord at that point in his life. I gained a whole new level of respect for him that day. He has been there for me during crisis in my life, like the passing of my brother, and did not hold it against me when I failed to make it to his mother's funeral because of my obligations. Our relationship's value increased dramatically and it all began when he canceled the debt I owed. He allowed me to do justice and make repairs. I canceled his debt and he went into damage control. To this day, I consider him a true friend and brother.

## To the perpetrators of pain

Those of you who are in debt to people because of the damage you have inflicted must make the effort to clear your heart. First, you must receive God's forgiveness for your part in wounding another person. Be brutally honest about what you have done. Some of you have committed incest, date rape, seduced a man or woman, manipulated, lied, gossiped, back-stabbed, physically beaten someone, or stolen money. Do not try to pursue a relationship with the victim. Most of you may not even be able to. Please get wise pastoral, legal, or some other professional counsel on how to get released from what you have done. For now, you must forgive yourself. The nugget is the same for you. You cannot repair the damage until you cancel the debt you have on your own heart and soul. Until you do this, you will always perceive people as critics. People will make helpful suggestions and it will feel like you are being criticized all the time. This is because of the unforgiveness you have towards yourself.

## Single to marriage transition...

Now for those of you who are looking for your spouse, these principles are extremely important. Carol and I have ministered to couples preparing for marriage for over ten years. Even if it was their second marriage, it always came down to these issues: Judgment, Justice, and Equity. You must deal with your potential mate in these areas before you ever stand at the altar and say, "I do". During the exciting and romantic time, when things are coming together for the big wedding day, you must make judgments, do justice and apply equity. We strongly recommend pre-marital classes, books, and teaching through your local church leadership.

Carol and I have been married since December of 1980. After a few years of debt cancellations and damage control, our relationship has a value that is second only to our relationship with Jesus Christ. We desire the same for you, but it takes walking according to this nugget of wisdom about relationships.

Chapter

# 4

# Readiness
## *All Degreed Up and No Where to Go*

## Chapter 4

"To give prudence to the simple, to the young man knowledge and discretion" (Proverbs 1:4)*

## Purpose of God

HEAR A JUST CAUSE O' LORD HEAR MY CRY
GIVE AN EAR TO A PRAYER FROM LIPS THAT WON'T LIE
LET JUDGEMENT ON MY LIFE
COME FORTH FROM YOUR PRESENCE
LET YOUR EYES SEE MY HEART AND GET BELOW THE SURFACE
TRY MY HEART LORD, GIVE ME VISITS IN THE NIGHT
YOU HAVE TESTED ME AND FOUND NOTHING WRONG,
AINT THAT RIGHT
I HAVE KEPT MY FEET FROM THE PATH OF THE VIOLENT MAN
FOLLOWED HARD AFTER YOU, NO SLIPPIN', I'LL STAND

I PRAY THAT THE GOD OF OUR LORD JESUS CHRIST
WOULD FILL YOU WITH THE SPIRIT OF WISDOM AND MIGHT
OF THE REVELATION KNOWLEDGE OF HIM I DECREE
AND I PRAY THAT THE EYES OF YOUR HEART WOULD SEE
SO THAT YOU MAY COME TO KNOW
OF THE HOPE OF HIS CALLING,
INHERITANCE OF THE SAINTS AND THE RICHES OF THE GLORY
ONE MORE THING THAT YOU GOTTA RECEIVE
IS THE GREATNESS OF HIS POWER TOWARD US WHO BELIEVE

I'M IN THE PURPOSE OF GOD
AND I'VE BEEN PURCHASED BY GOD
CAUSE I'M NOT WORTHLESS TO GOD.
HE'S MADE A CLAIM ON ME
AND SINCE I'M SPECIAL TO GOD, I'LL BE A VESSEL OF GOD
BECAUSE HE'S WRITTEN HIS NAME ON ME

- Chris Green, Heart of the Nation Music 1998

**73**

Proverb 1:4 is one of the most exciting verses in this entire proverb. To grasp a deeper meaning let's uncover some definitions of key words:

**Prudence:** to have understanding, it is practical wisdom, having wise management of your affairs. It suggests quickness of apprehension, the penetrating consideration that precedes action.

**Simple:** naïve, unsuspecting

**Knowledge:** Education, Frame-of-Reference, Teaching

**Discretion:** Perception, Tact, and Courtesy "to have understanding" (4)

I will take some liberty and paraphrase it like this: This proverb was written to give practical wisdom and the ability to wisely manage your affairs. Wisdom gives someone who is naïve and unsuspecting the ability to consider one's actions. It provides for the young man (or woman) an education and a frame of reference for navigating through life with perception and tact. This verse means one is prepared. It means wisdom can make you ready for life. Life can be very unpredictable. Unless you are ready for it, you will be chasing rather than leading, always a day late and a dollar short. I believe God wants you ready for life. He wants you ahead of the game and anticipating the next move rather than always cleaning up after another spill.

One of the couples in our ministry was going through a contemplative season in their life. They were in their mid-twenties and had been married almost five years. They are like a son and daughter to us and we had talked about it, but they could not find the words to describe how they were feeling. One Sunday morning as we spoke to each other briefly, they told me they had the words to describe the season. They called it a time of evaluation. With so many decisions to make for their future, they wanted to know if all their education and experiences were adding up to anything. There was serious questioning if all they had gone through was worth it.

Instantly a thought came to me and I blurted out these words. "All you have gone through and experienced to this point in your life has prepared you for the decisions you must make today. Nothing has gone to waste!" They looked at me and said; "Now that is a word of wisdom from God." When you are living by God's designs, every success or failure, every downfall or promotion has a purpose. Nothing goes to waste. If you do not want to waste time and life, then you must live by design.

## All Dressed Up and No Where to Go

Life seems to take us through long periods of preparation. We hit a stall where we feel like we are all dressed up but have nowhere to go. We have agonized with many who have graduated from college, but they cannot seem to find ANYTHING in their field of training. I cannot tell you how many have found themselves as teacher assistants or secretaries (administrative assistants...excuse me) and it was the very thing they tried desperately to avoid. I believe God takes us through these times of training and preparation before allowing us to step into destiny. This preparation is in our heart. We can have a lot of head knowledge and information, but our hearts are not ready for the next level. God uses these times to purify our motives and adjust our strategy. He makes us confront self-esteem issues and pride. It is not just life's coincidences, but it is God's way of putting us right in line with His designs for our life. God's designs are much more than just what we will do with our life. His designs involve working on WHO we will be. That is why He will humble you and break you down through a minimum wage job even though you may have a college degree. He makes us face our prejudice against others by putting us in lowly positions. God will even tell you sometimes to volunteer your professional services rather than always taking pay for your skill. You see, in God's Eternal Designs, no task, title or person can be beneath you. He will make sure you do not see your talents and abilities solely as a means to make money.

## Life is a marathon, not a sprint; pace yourself.

God makes us go further than saying with our lips that we are walking humbly before Him and with others. He will actually make us live it out. Not for just a month or two, but for years. I know this is a tough pill to swallow, but it is a necessary one. It may be many years before you get to do what you actually went to school for, trained for, or dreamed of. The Bible is full of examples. Don't let pride make you think you are an exception to the rule. Moses tried to get started at 40. It did not happen until he was 80. Joseph was dreaming at 17, but those dreams did not come true until he was 30. Even Jesus Christ was fired up at 12, but He submitted to the process of His Father's eternal designs. He worked with his earthly family and we do not read anymore about Him until He was 30 years old. I did not write this to depress you, but to temper and encourage you. Pace yourself. Life is a marathon, not a sprint. Stop the fleshly motivated rush and calm down. Submit your life and plans to God right now. Take a deep breath and just surrender your whole being into the sovereign hand of God. Take this nugget of wisdom and say to God, "Lord, whatever you want to do with me, and however you want to take me through life, is fine with me. I give my future to you."

As this issue is settled in your heart, you can hear and receive God's NOW in the upcoming pages without getting filled with anxiety or frustration.

## Living By Design

I believe in order for you to be ready for life, you must live with intent and purpose. If you allow anything to come your way, then that is exactly what happens, anything! If you are waiting for something to happen then that is exactly what you will get. Not what you want or need, but something! You have to live according to a plan and a design. Let's take a look at some of the basic meanings of the word, design. I found at least five definitions:

1) To make preliminary sketches of, to sketch a pattern or outline

2) To plan and carry out by artistic arrangement or in a skilled way

3) To form plans in the mind

4) To plan to do, purpose, to intend

5) To set apart for some purpose

So by these definitions this topic could be explained as: Living by a pattern, an outline, a plan, artistic arrangement and skill, intention, and set apart for a purpose.

Our quest is to find the design that will bring victory, success, and fulfillment. Let's put the topic in the form of these questions:
Living by whose pattern? Living by whose outline? Living by whose plan? Living by whose artistic arrangement and skill? Living by whose intention? Living set apart for who's purpose? The obvious answer is God, but are you willing to accept His design for your life?

"A manufacturer lets the product's intended use govern the design"- Dr. Myles Munroe - The Pursuit of Purpose.

### "What does God want you to be when you grow up?"

What is God's intended use for you? It is directly connected to His designs for your life. Most of us catch a glimpse of some superstar athlete or entertainer and we hold on to the mental picture and cherish it as our very own dream. Never once do we ask God if it is what He wants us to do. Sometimes our family pushes us to take on certain professions. We cave in under the pressure and set out to be a doctor, accountant, lawyer or preacher without ever asking God what is His design for our life. How many times did some adult ask you, "What do you want to be when you grow up?" Did anyone ever ask you, "What does God want you to be when you grow up?"

I believe another misunderstood verse in the Bible is Proverbs 16:1, which says "The plans of the heart belong to man, but the answer of the tongue is from the Lord. It goes on to say in verse 9, "a man's heart plans his way, but the Lord directs his steps."*

Most interpret this to mean we personally come up with the plans and afterwards, God will step in and show us how to accomplish our plan. First of all, the word **plans** actually means preparations. It could read as follows: **The preparation of the heart belongs to man.** God expects us to do whatever is necessary to prepare our hearts to receive the answer of the tongue. You see, you and I cannot come up with the answer to the question about our future. You cannot look at your gifts and talents and receive all the answers. Our gifts and talents can be indicators of our purpose. They can give us a clue or a glimpse of what we are going to do with our lives, but too many of us make the mistake of determining our future based purely upon what we know about ourselves. The problem with this method of determining our future is that there are hidden gifts and talents within us. You may set out to do and be something that is only half of your full potential. Carol and I are living proof of this.

### There was a songwriter/ singer inside of me

When we began our Sunday services at Metro Christian Worship Center in 1988, Pastor Raphael asked us to oversee the teen ministry of the church. I flatly refused the request. I did not like rap music. I did not feel qualified to minister to young people. According to my knowledge about myself, none of my gifts had anything to do with teenagers. Finally in 1992, we accepted the position as youth pastors in our church. We were totally out of our comfort zone. We were in the perfect position to have God tap into talents and gifts we did not know we had. We felt we could not relate to the young people, so God gave us creativity to reach them. God gave us music in our dreams. Ideas came for skits. Suddenly creativity was coming out of the young people as well and we found ourselves relating to them through music and the performing arts. We never had aspirations of music or singing, but we found ourselves leading teenagers in praise, worship and music outreach. By the time we trained new leaders to take our place, we had written over 50 songs, produced tapes and CD's, a couple of musical dramas and started a dance/pep team. If I had pursued only the areas of my technical gifting in radio and television production, I would never have discovered there was a songwriter/ singer inside of me also. The first step in making this discovery was in the preparation of my heart. I had to humble myself and submit to the direction God was placing right in front of me. Many times we reject the doors that are opened to us because they don't seem to lead to what we desire to do with our lives.

## Giving God a clean slate

Jeremiah 4:2 says, for thus says the Lord to the men of Judah and Jerusalem: **"Break up your fallow ground**, And do not sow among thorns." * I had to break up the hardness in my heart that was rejecting God's designs and plans for me. The preparation of the heart involves preparing the soil of our heart to receive the word (seed) and plans of God. Like me, you may have to lay aside your plans. It is like taking an eraser and wiping away all the writing on a board. You have to present to God a clean slate.

Proverbs 16:9 (a man's heart plans his way, but the Lord directs his steps. *) took on a whole new meaning in my life. With all the plans I had in my heart, the Lord directed my steps so that my plans were adjusted, fine-tuned, and brought into perfect synchronization with the designs He had for my life.

The answer of the tongue does come from God, especially for those who offer Him a prepared heart. God can give you the answer of the tongue about your career, ministry, or spouse if you take the time to prepare your heart. In your transitional twenties, people are always asking you about your future plans. When someone ask you 'What are you going to do now?' the answer comes from God, not the determinations in your heart. The answer of the tongue is from the Lord **because He fills in the blanks**.

Many of you are familiar with a certain parable told by Jesus Christ about a sower and seeds falling on different types of soil. I took the liberty to replace the word seed with the word designs so I could help you grasp the importance of being prepared. It would read like this from Mark 4:

"Listen! Behold, a sower went out to sow (designs). And it happened, as he sowed, that some **designs** fell by the wayside; and the birds of the air came and devoured it. Some **(designs)** fell on stony ground, where it did not have much earth; and immediately it sprang up because it had no depth of earth.  But when the sun was up it was scorched, and because it had no root it withered away. And some **designs** fell among thorns; and the thorns grew up and choked it, and it yielded no crop. But other **designs** fell on good ground and yielded a crop that sprang up, increased and produced: some thirty-fold, some sixty, and some a hundred. And He said to them, "He who has ears to hear, let him hear!" *.

**Education and training are a part of your preparation.**

This principle of **waiting for** God's answer runs the risk of sounding like you do nothing but sit around passing time while God does everything for you. I am not saying that. As one who dropped out of college, I am a strong advocate for young people to finish high school and get as much education or training as they possibly can. Even if you did not finish high school, get your G.E.D. (A program offered in American education to earn the equivalent of a high school diploma). Go to a community college, trade school, technical school, Bible College, or attend workshops and seminars. You can pick up training through your employer.

For those of you who have completed your college education, this advice sometimes becomes difficult to receive because you may feel it is time for your reward due to your labor over the years. You feel you have earned the right to start making some money and real success. To some measure, you have earned that right, but when you graduated, they called it a commencement exercise. Commencement means beginning. They were telling you the truth. It was the beginning of another level of education. College was preparation for where you are now. I think of it like this. Education gave you information. Training is application. After graduation you still need some training. I say this because even without the degree, I found myself sitting beside college graduates getting training with companies. My education and training has continued through weekend workshops and seminars as well as lessons in life skills. I have earned two certificates through the University of Missouri's Continuing Education Outreach Program. Carol and I completed a five year Discipleship and Leadership Training Program in our local church. What we missed through a four-year university, we still got through fifteen years of hard knocks, lessons, and programs. I still recommend formal education, but know that whatever academic level you obtain, it is preparation of your heart for God's designs for your life. You are always in the education

**81**

(school) of life. You are always preparing yourself to receive the answer of the tongue. Remember, it is the responsibility of man to prepare his own heart. Education and training (academically, physically, emotionally, mentally, and spiritually) are a part of your preparation. The moment you feel like you have learned, trained, and worked enough, it is an indicator your heart is not prepared to receive the next answer of the tongue. We are always seeking to know the next step. Your preparations now, are getting you ready for the next answer.

## The perfect material for God

Never take **a word from God** regarding your life lightly or irreverently. I believe there is a creative element released for our purpose and destiny. When you pray and ask God what you are supposed to do, you will receive an answer. Just wait a moment or two before going off with your own thoughts. This is difficult for those of us who are impatient. This process makes us feel lazy and irresponsible. Why do we think waiting for a word from God will mean we will sit and accomplish nothing? How can a word from God come into your life and it result in nothing? According to Genesis 1:2 and John 1, the Word was present at the beginning of this world, creating from nothing and making all that exist. Here is the nugget of wisdom for your life. When you empty your heart and prepare your soil, it is like giving God nothing to work with, which is the perfect material for Him. It is one thing to give God a set of plans and ask Him to bless them, but I believe the most powerful aspect of God is released when you sacrifice your own ideas and ask Him to create something new within you. When you say, "Lord, I am like the earth in the beginning. I am void and empty and darkness covers my deep places. Speak over my life, Lord. Let there be light over me. Make a whole new world out of my life. Create something that has never existed before and do it inside of me. I submit to your design for my life." Only when you come to this place do you begin to understand that God is not only bringing out the gifts within you, but His focus is the gift that He makes out of you.

## Get your G.E.D. (God's Eternal Design)

Sometimes people who missed academic lessons and classes the first time go back and get them again. As I previously mentioned, in America, if one fails to graduate from high school, they can earn a G.E.D (General Education Diploma). They can get the information they missed and thus get the opportunity to make things right. When it comes to God's purpose, you can have a doctorate level of earthly education, but still have missed His lessons and classes. You must go back to get God's Eternal Designs (G.E.D.).

I believe designs are the practical application of purpose like wisdom is the practical application of knowledge. We do not really know what to do with our gifts until we get God's word (designs). Some of you are planning to earn an engineering degree and then a high paying position somewhere, but God plans to use you as an urban schoolteacher. Some of you are in medical school planning for your own medical practice, but God plans to use you in missions and outreach. Some of you can speak three languages and plan to work at the United Nations, but God wants you to be an interpreter for a local pastor who has a multi-ethnic membership. Some of you are powerful singers and songwriters who plan to travel all over the world, but God wants you to sing and write for children's ministries and record nursery rhymes to save a new generation. This is what I mean by having a G.E.D. (God's Eternal Designs). Like the whole world, you can become so money and fame driven you associate your life's work only with those occupations that will bring wealth and notoriety. You can quote scriptures about being the head and not the tail. You can declare you are above and not beneath. You can say you are more than a conqueror, but have no concept that true success is obedience to God. True blessing is walking in the will and plans of God for your life.

Your self-esteem can be so attached to your own concepts of success that you can actually refuse to walk in the will of God. You will find it difficult to receive God's will as being anything other than the image you cherish for your future. I believe God is seeking to release a generation that will truly seek His heart and not just His hand. God wants a generation that will embrace the true G.E.D.

## The shortest distance between two points

We are taught, in Geometry, the shortest distance between two points is a straight line. I have discovered in life, the shortest distance between two points is not necessarily a straight line. The shortest distance is actually obedience to God. The most direct path may seem like the shortest distance on the surface, but only God knows it will actually lead to a ten-year detour of your destiny. God reserves the right to tell you the shortest route between where you are now and where you are going may involve stopping in places and working with people that are not in your route plans. He knows the way He sends you will take you across the path of people, events, and resources you will need when you arrive at your destination. You must trust God with your future. You must trust Him with **the path and the process** to get you there. **You must trust His design for your life**.

Chapter

# 5

# Revelation
*Who told you so?*

## Chapter 5

A wise man will hear and increase learning, And a man of understanding will attain wise counsel, (Proverbs 1:5) *

### A warning is a warning, not a weak opinion

Everybody has advice for someone in the transitional twenty something season. How do you know who is right and who is wrong? If someone advises you to make a certain decision, how do you know it is the right one? One of the tragedies that hit the music community was the death of the young 22-year-old entertainer Aalyah. From what I understood from the news reports, the plane crash that took her life was avoidable. The plane was overloaded with equipment and flown against the advice of those who had a better understanding of flying that type of aircraft. Aalyah may not have made the actual decision, but someone did and it cost everyone on the plane their life. I am not criticizing anyone. What is my point? This is another nugget for your life.

When people give you advice that involves going against the laws of nature or God don't take it! There were people who understood the laws of aerodynamics and physics as well as the design of the airplane. They had knowledge and experience to back them up. These are two things most people ignore all the time: knowledge and experience. The argument against flying in an overloaded plane was not just a personal opinion or an overprotective suggestion. Too many times, humans defy the advice given to them because they do not take warnings for what they are. A warning is a warning, not a weak opinion. Maybe it is because they have been able to get away with breaking laws. Some of you may have gotten away with speeding in your car, cheating on test, driving drunk, sleeping around without getting someone pregnant, or taking extra time off from the job without getting caught.

## Taking off in an overloaded plane

Often, people feel they can break the rules because frankly, they have done it before. If you are one of them, all you have done was just over loaded your airplane. Every experience was an extra piece of luggage brought on board. That is why every time you get away with something it is tougher to get away with the next thing. It is like, repeatedly, taking off in an overloaded plane and making the weight heavier and heavier each time. Eventually, it is going to crash! That is why, as a pastor over young people, I spoke against pre-marital sex and homosexuality. I do not hate those that practice these things. It is simply that these issues violate the laws of nature and God. The human body and spirit were not made to have multiple partners. You were not made to engage in sex outside of the covenant bond of marriage or in same sex practices. These are verifiable medical facts. When you overload your airplane by defying this warning, eventually, it will crash.

I cannot forcibly keep anyone from overloading their plane with experiences, ideas and arguments against my advice. Yet, I must admit that I am broken hearted to know that anyone would knowingly and willingly overload their plane and attempt to defy these emotional, medical, and spiritual aerodynamic laws. It always, eventually, ends in a crash. Just do not label me as a basher or a hater because I stand at the runway of so many lives telling young people, in particular, "You have overloaded your plane with ideas and concepts that the laws of nature and God are not going to support when you try to take off in your life." Since I love young people, I have to tell them. If I were a true basher or hater, I would be silent and just let them crash. My silence would say that I would rather see them dead instead of flying and soaring.

I must add this for the sake of those activist groups who are accusing pastors of bashing people. I am not targeting any particular people group in issuing this particular warning. During our teen ministry years I obtained information from the Medical Institute for Sexual Health from Austin, Texas. They outlined various consequences of sex outside of marriage between a man and a woman. In his books "Sex and the Bible" and "Sex is A Spiritual Act", Dr. Dale Conaway points out there is much more involved than the physical aspects of sex. There are emotional and spiritual dynamics taking place also. Therefore it is not heterosexual or homosexual bashing to point out the consequences of violating these spiritual and physical laws. I am addressing this so strongly because we have had to cry with too many young adults who discovered they were pregnant, HIV positive or had contracted some other disease. I pray that this bit of revelation will help you make some wise choices.

## How do I know if what I am hearing is right or wrong?

In the transitional twenty something season, you must be willing to hear and increase in learning. This was always difficult for me because it led me to one question. How do I know if what I am hearing is right or wrong? I believe this question has only one answer. You and I must learn how to recognize the voice and will of God for our life. I must give you the wisdom my pastor and brother, Raphael Green, taught us. There are specific ways you can discern if a thought, feeling, dream, supernatural occurrence, person, or even a book you read, is God speaking to you. There are at least three ways to identify the voice and will of God.

## How do you know God is speaking to you?

There are some very important questions you must ask if you really want to know if what you are experiencing or hearing is from God.

In our home church in St. Louis, we were taught that faith involves three key elements. These elements **are insight from God, agreement with God, and obedience to God**. When you have these three elements operating in any matter or action, you will find you are walking in faith, discerning the voice and will of God.

The first area, **insight from God**, means you must learn to discern if the idea or view that you have is from God. No matter what you are doing or saying, you are not in Biblical faith if it did not come from God. This statement automatically carries us into some very important questions we must ask.

## 1. Is this in harmony with the Word of God?

Obviously this means you must have solid Biblical teaching. Steer clear of only living by personal interpretation of scripture. Get connected with a reputable pastor and church in your community. Get grounded in balanced and sound teaching of the word of God. By balanced, I mean there should be emphasis on more than just one or two topics in the Bible. In our home church in St. Louis, every member is instructed in everything from basic Bible teachings (salvation, baptism, faith, prayer) to more advanced subjects like the Kingdom of God and Leadership Training for your home, community and church. Balanced teaching will lay the foundation necessary to judge whether something you are reading, hearing, or experiencing is in harmony with the Bible. If it is **not** in agreement with what the Bible teaches, you know that **it is not from God** no matter how logical or spectacular it may be. Sometimes things move us emotionally, but it is still not in agreement with the word of God. I grew up in and around church life. There were scores of songs that moved us emotionally, but the lyrics were not in line with what the Bible actually says or means. Many of those songs were not in harmony with the will of God. You should always apply this question to anything you believe God wants you to do or say. Is this in harmony with the Word of God? Is there a scripture (properly interpreted) to back it up?

All of my life I have heard scriptures in the Bible quoted out of context. The mass media does it all the time in sitcoms, commercials, and movies. Since many of us do not know the Bible very well, we actually live according to the world's interpretation of Bible scriptures. This is probably the most difficult issue that I have to address in this book because we have been trained to interpret all of life against our experiences. Therefore we see no need to go any further than surface, superficial knowledge of the Bible to determine the course of our life. You and I must have a more accurate interpretation of the Bible to walk out this principle. Don't just find a scripture that sounds close to what you want to do. Instead you must find out if that scripture, when used in its proper context, really means what you are saying. If you say you love your mother, and you love your dog, do you mean you have the same kind of love for your mother as you do for your dog? Of course not. The word love has a different meaning in the context of those two statements. That is what I mean by determining the proper context of a scripture. You must interpret according to the proper context so that you are not giving the wrong meaning to a scripture. Then you can begin to see if what you think God is saying for you to do is in harmony with the Bible. You should be able to find your answers to these kinds of questions in the word of God, verbatim (exactly word for word answers) or in the principles presented. This is the most important question to ask in determining if God is speaking to you.

## 2. Is the peace of God present?

Whenever something is done in agreement with God's word, the inner witness of the Holy Spirit or the peace of God will be present. This can be described as an inward certainty. Romans 5:1 states, "Therefore, having been justified by faith, we have peace with God through our Lord Jesus Christ" * Romans 8:14 says,

"For as many as are led by the Spirit of God, these are sons of God. For you did not receive the spirit of bondage again to fear, but you received the Spirit of adoption by whom we cry out, 'Abba, Father.' The Spirit Himself bears witness with our spirit that we are children of God." * Romans 15:13 says, "Now may the God of hope fill you with all joy and peace in believing, that you may abound in hope by the power of the Holy Spirit."* From these three passages you can see how the **inner witness** is that **same peace and certainty** that you received when you committed your life to Jesus Christ. The same peace and certainty of your salvation and justification is the same peace that lets you know if something you are facing is of God. You could think of it like this. Colossians 3:15 says: "And let the peace of God rule in your hearts, to which also you were called in one body; and be thankful". * The peace of God will be like an official in a sporting event who tells you if something is fair, foul, safe, or out. This guidance is necessary so that we do not operate out of our feelings. If we are in harmony with the word of God, **the peace of God will be present** to let you know that you are on target.

In our pre-marital advice to couples we have faced many situations where the couple told us they had a peace from God about their marriage. Such statements, in some cases, disturbed us where the couple was in clear violation of the principles of the Bible. What we would later discover was that their peace was based upon high salary potential and knowing the kind of lifestyle they could have if they combined their income. Their peace was based on getting away from parents or covering up a pre-marital pregnancy. Their peace was based upon anticipated sexual gratification or the dream coming true of a storybook wedding. This is not what is meant by the peace of God. It is not a calm feeling that everything will be all right. It is not adding up the numbers and figuring out how to make things work economically. There is a natural resolve that anyone can and will have when dates, times, schedules, and budgets can be met. This is not necessarily the peace of God. These things are not the same **as the inner certainty**. What if you have everything in place, but there is still no inner certainty or assurance? The nugget of wisdom here is to go back to question # 1. **Is this in harmony with the Word of God?** Don't ever allow positive circumstances or possibilities determine "a peace" about what you desire to do. Circumstances will change, but the inner certainty will remain the same.

### 3. Is Jesus Christ being glorified or revealed through this?

Who is going to look good when everything is over, God or me? This is a hard question, but a very necessary one. This takes being honest. Our plans are always self-centered. No matter how much we say we just want to help people or do things that others may be touched, the bottom line is we want credit for it. When words and deeds are really of God, you can rest assured that He will do it in such a way that we cannot take credit for it. I wrestle with this daily because I want some hint of recognition for my accomplishments. I want somebody to recognize that God told me to do this. I want somebody to see my sacrifices. I want someone to know what I did in secret. The truth is that often when it is of God, nobody will see you. Only Jesus will get the glory. This question deals with our motivation. When we say that God has shown or given us something to say or do, if the bottom line is self glorification, we can take a legitimate Godly experience and turn it into a fleshly, carnal display of selfishness and pride. This last question forces us to really consider two things; If this is really what God wants me to do and I get a negative response, am I willing to obey Him anyway? If I get a glorious and wonderfully received response, am I willing to humble myself and quickly turn all the attention to Jesus?

### Some dreams will never come to pass

Another reason you need to receive revelation is so you can be ready and able to face the many uncertainties of life. In spite of all the plans, hopes, and dreams you may have, you still have no way of knowing how your life is going to actually unfold. There are many things already in motion, which are inevitably going to affect you. The economic, political, and social dynamics of our world will be a part of shaping your future. I am in no way discounting the sovereignty of God. It's just that these become factors in revealing how some things were never meant to be for your life.

America experienced the worst terrorist attack in the nation's history on September 11, 2001. Millions of lives have been dramatically and traumatically changed since that day. Undoubtedly, many of you have been impacted in some way also. It may have been by way of family, friends, co-workers, church groups, or the television. But make no mistake, a series of events have been set in motion leading to several serious changes in your life. For some of you, your job and income may have changed. You may have been called to active duty in the military. There are some people who may have dreamed of owning a business in the World Trade Center, but like many dreams that you may have had, this will never come to pass. Things have changed forever and will never be the same for them, you or me.

In the Bible, Daniel and his three companions never expected to find themselves captured by another nation. This was their September 11th type experience. They had to learn a new language, a new culture and a whole new way of life. Undoubtedly all of their dreams and plans were shattered. The issue though is that God, in His sovereignty, had a plan all along. These four young men lived according to this nugget of wisdom during the worst transition of their lives; A wise man will hear and increase learning, and a man of understanding will attain wise counsel, Proverbs 1:5 * Just like these young men, you have to be able to face the unexpected. You still have to discern the voice and will of God in the midst of chaos and confusion. In the book of

Daniel you can see how they constantly prayed and asked God, "What do we need to do next? What do we need to do NOW?"

## I'm So Confused

A statement was made, "Knowledge is power." This is very true, but life has taken some unexpected turns and more than ever, you need revelation and not just information to face the future. A person of understanding is one who attains (reaches for) wise counsel. That counsel begins with learning **the Word of God**. That counsel is acted upon with obedience to **the God of the Word**.

**The second element of faith is agreement with God**. If you are going to live by revelation, you must be in agreement with God. This second element of faith is where most of us blow it. We find a scripture, quote it, tote and than then try to jump into element number three (obedience to God). The problem is that we really are not obeying God if we are not in agreement with Him. Many times we come into agreement with each other over a scripture, but that still is not agreement with God. As I pointed out in Chapter four, Readiness, we do not dictate to God how things should be done. I cannot recall how many times people asked us to pray for them because they were confused about God's direction for their lives.

As we have advised young people through the years, one theme repeatedly surfaces as a major source of confusion. It has been the failures to agree with God on what He is telling them do RIGHT NOW. They focus on the future, but stumble in the present. One of the major areas of confusion has been in the planning and implementing of their life's goals. From education to career advancement, scores have used the same words to describe their frustration. "I don't know what God wants me to do." When Carol and I have pushed and prodded a little, we have found that in most cases, they knew what they were supposed to do. They just did not want to do it. What they are presently supposed to do often involves simple life principles they do not want to adhere to. We advise people to never quit a job until you have already found another one. You never buy a new car on a part time or temporary income. Never make two major loans for big purchases at the same time (i.e. a house and a car) unless you can really afford it. Never enroll in extra classes just to finish school faster. The list goes on. When people violate these kinds of simple life principles, they get burned out emotionally, mentally, financially, and spiritually. They find themselves in a whirlwind of distress and doubt unable to hear what God wants them to do. They pray and pray, but God does not seem to answer. They ask others to pray for them and still God does not seem to answer. Could it be that God will not tell them anything else until they do what He has already told them?

How is your communication line with God right now? Is it quiet? His silence is not to confuse you. It just means you have not come into agreement with Him. The confusion will fade away as soon as you get back to what you already know you are supposed to do. Get back to agreement with God.

## The Road to Gaza (Obedience to God)

The third element of faith is obedience to God. Philip, a New Testament evangelist, was told by the spirit of God to go to the road that leads from Jerusalem to Gaza. When he got to that road, God directed him to an Ethiopian eunuch who was in his chariot reading scripture that he could not understand. Philip struck up a conversation and led the man into a personal relationship with Jesus Christ. I marveled at how Philip demonstrated all three elements of the faith walk. He received a word from God to go to the road that leads to Gaza (Insight from God). He agreed with God and obeyed. Once he got to the road, God told him to go to the Ethiopian. Again, he agreed with God and obeyed. This was a special place of obedience at this point because Philip remained sensitive to the voice of God. He could have brushed off the tug of the spirit to go to the Ethiopian by saying, "No, God told me to go on the road to Gaza and that is what I am going to do." He could have kept right on walking until he arrived in Gaza. He would have been very frustrated at the silence from God. He would have been wandering around Gaza asking God, "Why did you send me here?" He would have made the kind of mistake we make so often when God gives us instruction. We don't want to stop and talk to the Ethiopian eunuchs that God is sending us to in the first place. What if God has told you to get on the road that leads to a certain career? That road may involve obtaining the education and training to reach that goal (Gaza). Can you receive this nugget? This is a tough one. Maybe God told you to get on the road that leads to Law, Medicine, Engineering, Counseling, Athletics, Politics, Music, or Media, but he never intended for you to actually arrive in Gaza. He has Ethiopian eunuch type appointments for you. There are people to meet and places to go. God did not say for you to go to Gaza. He said get on the road that leads there.

Let's examine what happened to Philip after he fulfilled His assignment (Obedience to God). From Acts 8:37 we can catch the conversion of the Ethiopian eunuch and what happens to Philip. "Then Philip said, "If you believe with all your heart, you may." And he answered and said, "I believe that Jesus Christ is the Son of God." So he commanded the chariot to stand still. And both Philip and the eunuch went down into the water, and he baptized him. Now when they came up out of the water, **the Spirit of the Lord caught Philip away**, so that the eunuch saw him no more; and he went on his way rejoicing. But **Philip was found at Azotus**. And passing through, he preached in all the cities till he came to Caesarea." *

What an amazing turn of events! I believe God will do the same for you. If you will come into agreement with Him and obey

Him, you will find that God will miraculously place you exactly where you are supposed to be. Some of us are so dogmatically focused on getting to Gaza that we will totally miss the will of God for our lives. Maybe God never intended for you to reach Gaza. Maybe His intention was the road that led to Gaza. In this season of transition, the emphasis is not on the destination. **It is on the journey**. There is a wonderful revelation about your life that God wants to give you. Don't miss it!

Chapter

# 6

# Riddles
## *When My World is Shaking*

## Chapter 6

"To understand a proverb and an enigma, the words of the wise and their riddles." (Proverbs 1:6) *

### How could a God of love allow such a horrible thing?

September 11th, 2001 left many people questioning God and doubting His love and reality. How could a God of love allow such a horrible thing to happen? It is hard to find an answer that will satisfy you in the center of your soul. More than ever, you need the wisdom of God to handle the riddles of life.

Proverbs 1:6 uses the word enigma. Enigmas are riddles. Riddles are very tough and difficult questions whose answers lead us to clever reasoning or entrapping conclusions. Often the person asking the questions already has a certain conclusion they want to present. If the one asking the question has your best interest in mind, they can use a riddle to help you through your own thought process to see their point of view. If the riddle is intended to damage you, they will ask questions to shake your basic beliefs and understandings about yourself or your life.

### Riddles can rock your world

In the Bible, Luke 22:31 quotes Jesus making this statement to Simon Peter, "And the Lord said, "Simon, Simon! Indeed, Satan has asked for you, that he may sift you as wheat". *Interestingly, one of the figurative meanings of the word sift is riddle. Jesus is telling us, through Simon Peter, one of Satan's ploys is to riddle you. The effects of riddles can be seen in other definitions such as to shake, quiver, vibrate, or to rock to and fro. In other words, these tough questions draw you into conclusions and reasoning

**105**

that shake or rock you.

I believe the first thing to consider before you try to answer a riddle is to ask the individual proposing it, "Why are you asking me this question?" Since the point of a riddle is to lead you or draw you to a certain conclusion, when you come to it, you will face the challenge of believing the answer as truth or rejecting it as a very clever lie. This is not easy. Especially when you can see some truth in the conclusion.

Here's a classic riddle: If a tree falls in the forest and there is no one around to hear it, does it make a sound when it hits the ground? Somebody will answer, "Of course it makes a sound!" But how do you know it makes a sound if no one was there to hear it? Whether your answer is yes or no, where is the truth in your conclusion? This is the kind of riddle that can shake foundational beliefs about time, space, and existence. Foundation shaking riddles come when tragedies like September 11th come into our lives. Why did God let this happen? How do you know you won't be next? They can really rock your world.

## Disappointments, devastation, decisions and destiny

Riddles usually follow disappointments that are devastating. Whenever disappointment reaches this level, it usually involves something we believe God could have or should have changed.

Six months after the fateful September 11th tragedies, I was sitting on the side of my bed weeping as Pat Robertson and the 700 Club showed an interview with the family of one of the lost pilots. The widow and now single mother described her pain like this. "I felt like my heart was being ripped out of my chest and I was alive and could feel every bit of the pain. My heart literally disintegrated" I was sobbing as she described a pain and closeness to Jesus Christ I could relate to because of what I had gone through in my family losses. She was living proof that in those deeply devastating and disappointing times, your only recourse is to trust the One who loves you. If you start down the dark path of questioning the integrity and sovereignty of God, you are separating yourself from the only One who can help you get through it.

Still, I believe God allows the riddles for the reasons He said to Peter in Luke 22: 32 "But I have prayed for you, that your faith should not fail; and when you have returned to Me, strengthen your brethren." * I believe God allows the riddles so our faith can be strengthened. So we, in turn, can strengthen our brothers and sisters.

The nugget of wisdom here is you have to learn how to make it through the seasons of disappointment and devastation. You have to get past the questions that you do not have answers for. You have to trust the answers God gives you. You have to trust God even with the answers He places on hold; in the silence that says, "I love you, but I cannot answer that question for you right now."

It can get awfully hard to trust God when in the back of your mind you are convinced He could have changed the circumstances. Why didn't you get the job? Why did you have that accident? Why did that special person have to die? Riddles can paralyze you with fear and insecurity about your future. You can get to the point where you will blatantly disobey God because you are not too sure of what He may allow you to go through.

## I wondered if God was going to allow us to be killed

At the request of my pastor and brother, Carol and I took a mis-

**107**

sions trip to Monrovia, Liberia in West Africa in February 2002 to be a part of the Liberia For Jesus Prayer Crusade. Still dealing with the residual pains and uncertainties from our family's bereavement and facing the blaring warnings from September 11th, I really did not want to go. I did not want Carol to go. Then I decided I would go alone because I did not want her in such a dangerous situation. In Monrovia, Liberia, they were still living in the aftermath of civil war and there was still fighting going on just a few miles outside the capital city. I wondered if God was going to allow us to be killed and use our martydom to stir our church to action. I wondered if only one of us would return and the testimony of either surviving spouse would serve as a rallying point for our children. I did not want Carol to go through such agony. I did not want my children to have to go through such pain. I did not want my mother to lose another child. I honestly was not afraid of dying. I was thinking about how the death of either Carol or myself would affect our families. All of these questions and worries made me realize I was being riddled. I was being shaken. Slowly I recognized that I was trying to control the destiny of Carol and my children. The Lord gently reminded me my life is in His hands. Whatever He allows, I have to trust Him. He always has the eternal viewpoint. I finally consented to Carol going with us. In spite of all the devastation of the past few years and months, I still had to trust God.


Our nation was going through transition from peacetime to wartime. In wartime, there are many things you do not take for granted. In this kind of mental and emotional transition it is very easy to live in fear and try to keep everything and everyone protected and close to you. I had to let go and let God. For the first time in my life I was brought face to face with the reality of how little I really believed and trusted God. When we got on those planes and traveled in and out of immigration check points and military barricades, I could hear the words of Jesus from Mark 8:35 "For whoever desires to save his life will lose it, but whoever loses his life for My sake and the gospel's will save it." *

## Course Changes/ Shattered Dreams

Riddles also come when God allows our plans to fail. When plans fail it always means making changes because a dream gets shattered. It means coming to terms with those things that were never meant to be.

This nugget of wisdom is that changing your course does not mean God made a change. It usually means we are being forced to face the fact we have been going in the wrong direction. I have watched people go through so many unnecessary trials and pains simply because they were being led by their own desires. What many believe is the pursuit of God is actually the pursuit of their own dreams. There was a television show called Fame. It depicted the lives of young people who were willing to make any sacrifice to pursue their dreams for fortune and fame. Though there were many positive things about the show, the one glaring message that came through was this: You have to be willing to do anything to reach your goal. This kind of attitude can be the one motivation and driving force to get you to the next level on the ladder to success. It can be a great source of strength and endurance to advance, but what happens when God Himself steps in and starts blocking your progress? No matter how many contacts you try to make, resumes you send out, or business / ministry calling cards you distribute, you just cannot seem to get the breakthrough you are looking for. You attend breakthrough conferences, workshops and seminars. You may have even received breakthrough words of encouragement and exhortation, but nothing ever happens. Some of you have gone from job to job and from church to church looking for your big break. In the midst of the searching, you and your family have gone through financial heartbreak and relational break ups, which creates long seasons of isolation. This has led to an onslaught of riddles and questions. This kind of intense opposition quickly brings you to the point where you cannot believe God ever had a plan for you in the first place. Go back to square one before you give up. Back in 1993 God gave me this song:

SQUARE ONE
WE WERE FACED WITH DEADLINES
BEFORE THE BILLS CAME DUE
WE ASKED FOR A MIRACLE FROM GOD,
BUT THE MORTGAGE FELL THROUGH
I KNOW WHAT THE BIBLE SAID, BUT STILL MY DREAM IS DEAD
I CONFESSED THE POSITIVE VERSE,
MERE WORDS THAT FELL TO EARTH

SQUARE ONE, DID I REALLY HEAR GOD'S VOICE
SQUARE ONE, UNDERSTAND WHAT HE SAYS
SQUARE ONE, HAVE I TOTALLY COUNTED THE COST
SQUARE ONE, DARED TO TRULY OBEY

SATAN BRINGS THE EVIL DEEDS.
DESTROYS AND STEALS WHAT'S OURS
BUT I THOUGHT THIS WAS A TRIAL
TO SHOW GOD'S OVERCOMING POWER
IS MY MOTIVE SELFISHNESS? MY INNER GOAL SIMPLY PRIDE
I WANT TO KNOW FROM THIS DAY ON,
HOW TO WALK BY GOD'S SIDE

SQUARE ONE, DID I REALLY HEAR GOD'S VOICE
SQUARE ONE, UNDERSTAND WHAT HE SAYS
SQUARE ONE, HAVE I TOTALLY COUNTED THE COST
SQUARE ONE, DARED TO TRULY OBEY

CHRIS GREEN, HEART OF THE NATION MUSIC 1993

## You need the favor of God on your life

One sure way to answer these kinds of riddles is to get back to the original thing God spoke over your life and to seek His wisdom on how to bring it to pass. This simply means taking your dream and submitting it. I have seen hundreds forfeit their purpose simply because they would not submit under the counsel and discipline of a local church and pastor. They wander from church to church and city to city looking for someone or some-thing to endorse, affirm, and support them. LISTEN TO ME CLOSELY: The only ones who will do that for you are your spir-itual parents (your pastors). Your lack of success is due mainly to your refusal to humble yourself under fathers, mothers, and mentors in the gospel. You may be more talented, more intelli-gent, more charismatic, and more gifted than your pastors, but God has set it up so that you need their extended hands guiding you as you grow, pointing fingers scolding you as you learn, and loving arms holding you when you are discouraged. You need their hands laid upon you to thrust you forth into your destiny. You need the favor of God on your life and God has chosen to bestow His favor in this particular way.

## Attacks of hopelessness

The Biblical definition of the word HOPE is a desire and an expectation based upon what God has revealed. There is great-ness in you that God is revealing everyday, but we often allow the riddles of Satan to steal the desire and expectation. It is a lit-eral attack of hopelessness. This attack is most effective when there are long delays and dry seasons in our life. Proverbs 13:12 says "Hope deferred makes the heart sick, But when the desire comes, it is a tree of life."* There are no words to describe the heartsick times in the twenty something years. It is hard to work past the overwhelming feeling in your gut saying you are not going to make it. A gnawing riddle and question keeps playing over and over again, "Is it really going to happen? Is God going to do it?"

When my heart got very low, I found it hard to keep going to church. The sermons did not seem to address my issues and no one seemed to be talking about what I was dealing with. At one such season I was attending Abundant Life Fellowship in St. Louis, Mo. I was stressed on my job and I was getting depressed. I was not tithing faithfully. We were struggling financially. Whenever I was in that mood, I would spend money on elec-tronic gadgets. I was on my way home from work one evening

**111**

and I felt like going on a big spending binge. I could just run up the charge cards and let it all fall apart. I was headed for bankruptcy anyway, so why not just go down in a blaze of games and glory. I was going to skip the mid week service, but God impressed me heavily to go to church anyway. I had enough sense and experience to follow God when He was moving on me that seriously, so I went. I arrived late and the pastor, Matthew Ferguson was speaking. He talked about how we get depressed and decide to just blow all of our money. We charge up our credit cards and file bankruptcy. I sat feeling like a giant spot light had been turned on me. I went up for prayer that night and got delivered from that destructive tendency in my life. Since then, I have never underestimated the need to go to church and get a word from God. Even if the message does not hit you between the eyes like it did for me that night, you still need to be exposed to "The words of the wise and their riddles." –Proverbs 1:6* God used Bishop Ferguson to save my life and maybe my marriage that night. When you drop out of a church for weeks at a time, I guarantee you are missing the very answers you are looking for. Though your pastor, leaders, and friends may be speaking words that do not make sense, this proverb says you must understand the words of the wise and their riddles. God is using these people to riddle you and sift you in a precious cleansing way. You may not like their questions and their statements, but they are shaking off the chaff and chains that are binding you up.

## Come up to a higher level of thinking

Sometimes ministers like my pastor, Raphael Green, are accused of speaking words that are too high and lofty for people. He tells our congregation (especially our teens) to get a dictionary. He is requiring that we come up to a higher level of thinking, not to impress people, but to get out of survivalist mentality and into overcoming faith. Many people, even in the church, are fans of the television show "Survivor" They come away from the program with an impartation to live like a survivor. God uses the riddles of the wise to elevate us to a higher level than just mere survival. This practical exercise of learning new words and expanding our vocabulary is forcing us to think higher and be better. We are not just survivors. We are conquerors! No, we are more than conquerors! We are over comers!

The riddles of the wise will not allow you to settle for mediocrity, wallow in self-pity, sink into depression or retreat in fear. The riddles of the wise strengthen you to face the riddles of life. Make up your mind to stop running away from them. The wise ones may be your parents, teachers, pastors, or friends. Do not run away from the people who love you and into the arms of those who only care about what they can take from you. The sifting that takers will give you will tear you down, but the sifting of the wise will build you up.

# Chapter
# 7

# Reverence

*Have You Ever Been in Love?*

## Chapter 7

The fear of the LORD is the beginning of knowledge, but fools despise wisdom and instruction. (Proverbs 1:7) *

### Have you ever been in love?

Now before you reflect on that no good so and so who hurt you after you gave them your heart, please hear me out. Often our disappointments and heartbreaks can make us forget what it was really like to be in love with someone.

In our initial college days of just getting to know each other, Carol and I were with a group of our friends. It was a Friday night and everyone was trying to decide what we were going to do after a long week of classes and studying. We were all still new to each other and in the early days, we were just discovering how different our backgrounds and upbringing were. After a little deliberation the group decided to go out to eat and then go to a disco. Everyone was in full agreement and ready to leave except one person, me. I came from a background that taught going to the disco was unacceptable for Christian young adults. Having never been one to follow the crowd, I was adamant in my refusal to go. Up to this point in our relationship, Carol was a little bit more interested in me than I realized. She watched me take a stand in my conviction and she made a decision in that moment that was monumental for our relationship. She realized that if she went along with the crowd, that it would negatively alter my opinion of her. I was not trying to be self righteous or holier than anybody else, but she saw where I was on that issue. Rather than taking a risk of losing a prospective relationship with me, she changed her mind and stayed behind. The rest of the young people went out leaving the two of us to spend an evening together talking and the rest is history.

## Relationships change your priorities

This was just a natural level of respect, reverence, and fear between a young man and young woman. How much more can be said about this kind of reverence and fear of God? This is a simple example of what is meant when I say we must live with reverence and fear of God. You care more about what He thinks about what you say and do than the rest of the crowd. His opinion of you and your actions matters more than everyone else, in the same manner Carol cared more about my opinion of her than her desire to go out with the group.

Does God's word matter more to you than your friend's words and your own feelings and views? The only thing that changes your priorities is relationships. For a brother you may change your plans. For a wife you will drop everything. For your niece or nephew, you will drive the extra mile to find the perfect gift. Relationships often determine priorities. How much more when it comes to our relationship with God?

## Reverence comes out of intimacy

We all have a need for intimacy. Most people think that intimacy and sex mean the same thing, but they don't. Sex is one expression of intimacy. What we all truly desire is to be known, understood, and accepted. That is what intimacy is all about. I have not changed subjects. I am still talking about reverence and the fear of God. We just don't think of the fear of God as being the same thing as having an intimate relationship with Him. Actually, intimacy with God comes out of reverence. Reverence comes out of intimacy. They go hand in hand.

## I realized that I did not have street smarts to make it

I was born and raised in the inner city of St. Louis, Missouri.

Growing up in a Godly home with Christian parents did not keep us from facing the harsh realities of inner city life. There were shootings, fights, gangs, violence, pornography and crime all around every minute of everyday. It is not long before you realize you need knowledge, information, and smarts to survive the streets. Just getting back and forth from home to school could be a major ordeal. As a young kid I realized I did not have street instincts. I did not have a quick, sharp tongue and I did not know street lingo, therefore it was always hard to keep up. You realize very early that if you cannot keep up, you will be run over. You begin to decide very early in life if this Jesus Christ, Christianity, and church thing, is going to really work for you. It is not a decision that you wait until you are a teenager to come to. You decide at five, six, eight, or ten years old. I don't know how, but God brought the book of Proverbs to my attention very early in life. Some of the first scriptures I remember reading were Proverbs and Psalms because they somehow made sense to me. God brought Proverbs 1:7 to me as early as 8 or 9 years old. The fear of the Lord is the beginning of knowledge, but fools despise wisdom and instruction. *

I realized that I did not have the street smarts to make it, so I had to rely upon the Lord. Since knowledge is power, that power and knowledge can also be used against you. God was able to get it through to my little young mind that since I did not have all the knowledge that it took to make it in the streets, if I started with the fear of the Lord, I would be ahead. The fear of the Lord is the **beginning** of knowledge. The gangs and child molesters had knowledge and know how, but since I had the Lord, I was in the **beginning** of knowledge. I would be operating in the foreknowledge of God. I would be living in the forethought of God. That did not mean I had information, but God would tell me what to do and what not to do before enemies could use their knowledge against me. I stayed, ahead of the game.

**119**

## God was my friend, my buddy, and my bodyguard

This may sound like an astounding revelation for such a young kid, but it was my actual outlook on life. To me, I was just doing what it took to survive the streets. This fear of the Lord was cultivated out of an actual relationship with the Lord. Outside of my family, I was a very quiet kid. I was constantly talking to God, sometimes even out loud. He was just my friend, my buddy, and my bodyguard. I spent so much time alone as a child that my parents would worry about me. I would spend endless hours writing, reading, and playing, but to me I was never alone. Jesus was always playing and talking with me as far as I was concerned. I talked to Him about everything. I hated being perceived as naive, even though I was, but with the *beginning of knowledge* in my arsenal, I had this secret advantage in life.


When I did start to venture out and grow up, I ran into the harshness and cruelty of adolescence. In that season I closed up and became withdrawn because my "friends" hurt me. I even talked to Jesus about that. I was not necessarily okay and healed, but He was my place of comfort and security. I cared more about what He thought about things than anyone else around me. All through high school I never followed the crowd. I did not care what the crowd thought. Yes, I felt like an outcast. I felt lonely. I longed for strong bonding, but nothing and no one could take the place of Jesus. When I failed at football and gave up on soccer, He was right there. When I struggled with sexuality and the hormone explosions of puberty, He was right there. He helped me discover that I was a writer. He drew me into the school choir where I found measures of acceptance and friendship among peers. I became a straight "A" student because God helped me with Chemistry, Biology, Algebra, and Social Studies. He was so intimately a part of every aspect of my life that I just seemed to always know what to do and how to do it ahead of time. People thought I was smarter than I really was. Teachers called me a sleeping genius. My English Literature teacher called one of my writings the greatest piece of literature that she

**120**

had ever read from any of her students in all her years of teaching. I knew the real deal though. The Lord had just simply spoken to me. I just wrote what He showed me. I wrote what He said to me.

Through the years, people have given me far more credit than I ever deserved. In college when I got away from this reverence and intimacy, my life fell apart. My true nature came to the surface. My true inabilities blazed to the forefront. In and of myself, I am a quitter, a coward, a lazy glutton, and a fool. As Proverbs 1:7b says "but fools despise wisdom and instruction."* I found myself living foolishly. So I strongly urge you to receive this nugget of wisdom, reverence for God, into your life.

People like Bill Gates, president of Microsoft, are making millions of dollars because knowledge is power. They are reaping the benefits of being postured to disseminate knowledge and information. With all their skill and ability, they are merely tapping into knowledge that already exists. As a Christian, you can tap into the word of God, which is discerning what He has already spoken. I'm taking you one step further. By emphasizing to you that the fear of the Lord is the beginning of knowledge I am revealing that you don't merely tap into knowledge and information that already exist. You are postured to receive the forethought of God, the wisdom behind the written word.

Most of you may not be like me. You may have the street smarts, book smarts, and great skills to make it on your own, but please know that somewhere down the line you will come to a season where you must have the beginning of knowledge. Some enemy is going to be so far ahead of you in knowledge, skill, and information that you won't stand a chance. You will have to have the forethought of God to get ahead and stay ahead. There is only one way to get the beginning of knowledge and that is to have the fear of the Lord. That fear (reverence) comes out of an intimate relationship with God.

## Your reverence for God will be demonstrated practically in your respect for authority in your life.

How will you know that you are really living in the fear of God? I believe one way will be by the respect you have for those in authority that you are around everyday. How do you respect your father? How do you respect your mother? How do you respect your manager, supervisor, or boss? How do you really feel about your teachers, pastors, mentors, and leaders? There may be many issues between you and parent(s). There may be many problems between you and leaders, but that is why we dealt with justice, judgment and equity in chapter three. If you really live in the fear of God, you will be more concerned about His view of your relationships with the people in your life. Take a moment and review that chapter before moving on.

The way you treat the authorities God sets in your life can be an indication of how you truly feel about Him. You could be unaware of anger against God for allowing you to be raised and taught by people who hurt you. When you encounter these same kinds of authorities, you respond out of feelings from the past.

When you are enraged over the police or you think you can say anything you want to an instructor, God sees your attitude toward His authority. When you can defy the Biblical advice of pastors and mentors or if you shrug off the attempts of parent(s) to get back into your life, see how it uncovers your heart toward God. God will not allow this nugget to be lofty impractical words in an ancient religious book. He brings it right into your world today. Now is the time to take seriously God's perspective of the authorities He placed in your life. Even for those who abused their authority and totally messed up your life with their actions and deeds, it is time to face, forgive, and get free from it.

Jesus said, "If you love me, you will obey my commands." This is a command. This is direction. This is the fear of the Lord. This is the beginning of knowledge for the rest of your life. This is what it means to be in love with God.

Have you ever been in love?

Chapter

# 8

# Results
*Reality is No TV Show*

# Chapter 8

In America, there is a strange trend toward a new category of entertainment called reality TV. People are capturing real life moments on home video cameras and sending them to television networks. We are constantly being shown horribly graphic events on television. Let me remind you, reality is not a TV show!

## The Unrealities of Life

Pastoring for ten years has taught me one thing about people who are going through transitions in life: Their expectations can be completely unrealistic. Carol and I have watched people transition from other cities into ours, move from another church into ours, move from one job into another, venture into marriage, or make their first steps into parenting. In these transitions, their expectations were completely unrealistic. They had unrealistic expectations of others and themselves.

For many years' people were frustrated, disappointed, and hurt by us as pastors because we could not always be there for them in critical transitional seasons. I watched people leave our church because the pastors could not (I did not say would not) be in two or three places at the same time. Even when they discovered that the pastors were away on emergencies or handling other serious matters, they still left the church. Sometimes I felt I had to start working on being omni-present.

Unrealistic expectations seem to be the result of an accumulation of disappointments and failings in one's life. As I mentioned in chapter three, Relationships, if you do not forgive yourself or others, you cause yourself or others to feel something is owed.

This sense of debt is because of your expectations. The standard of perfection is so high that it is like expecting people to be God in your life. The real deception is that you keep thinking that you are not expecting very much from people. I'm tell you that your expectation really is too high no matter how low you think it is. Once people fail to be there in ways only God can be there for you, the feelings of loss start all over again. The endless cycle of unrealistic standards continues.

Proverbs 1:8-19 gives what I call a list of life's realities. "My son, hear the instruction of your father, And don't forsake the law of your mother, For they will be a graceful ornament on your head, and chains about your neck. My sons, if sinners entice you, don't consent. If they say, 'Come with us, Let us lie in wait to shed blood; Let us lurk secretly for the innocent without cause; Let us swallow them alive like Sheol, And whole, like those who go down to the Pit; We shall find all kinds of precious possessions, We shall fill our houses with spoil; Cast in your lot among us, Let us all have one purse'— My son, don't walk in the way with them, Keep your foot from their path; For their feet run to evil, And they make haste to shed blood. Surely, in vain the net is spread in the sight of any bird; but they lie in wait for their own blood, they lurk secretly for their own lives. So are the ways of everyone who is greedy for gain; it takes away the life of its owners." *

Then the writer takes the time to give the results of failing to accept the realities of life. "Because I have called and you refused, I have stretched out my hand and no one regarded, Because you disdained all my counsel, And would have none of my rebuke, I also will laugh at your calamity; I will mock when your terror comes, When your terror comes like a storm, and your destruction comes like a whirlwind, when distress and anguish come upon you. Then they will call on me, but I will not answer; they will seek me diligently, but they will not find me. Because they hated knowledge and did not choose the fear of the LORD, They would have none of my counsel and despised my every rebuke. Therefore they shall eat the fruit of their own way, and be filled to the full with their own fancies. For the turning away of the simple will slay them, and the complacency of fools will destroy them." -Proverbs 1:23-32 *

## You may be where you are because you did not listen to wisdom

I believe that part of the reason God does not allow pastors, family, and friends to be there for some people at certain times in their life is because they are in a season of consequences. They are facing the results of decisions made in the past. They are dealing with the consequences of failing to heed the warnings of wisdom. This is a priceless nugget to embrace.

This chapter had to be included in this book because there are some places that you come to in life that are because of your own decisions. I will deal with those issues in which we were victims and we suffered due to the decisions and actions of others. For now, though, you must come face to face with the matters in which you can no longer point the finger at someone else. Stop blaming your parents for decisions that you made. Stop blaming pastors for your inconsistency. Stop blaming your boss or your co-workers for your bad attitude and stubborn disposition. You may be where you are because you did not listen to wisdom when it was being offered. Proverbs 1:20-23 makes it very clear that God gave you a chance to avoid the results you have right now.

"Wisdom calls aloud outside; She raises her voice in the open squares. She cries out in the chief concourses, at the openings of the gates in the city She speaks her words: "How long, you simple ones, will you love simplicity? For scorners delight in their scorning, and fools hate knowledge. Turn at my rebuke; surely I

129

will pour out my spirit on you; I will make my words known to you". *

One of my spiritual sons told me that he reminisces about the old days when he was in the teen ministry. Now that he is in his twenties, he wishes he had heeded the words and advice given to him in his teenage years. Many wonderful opportunities have passed him by because he did not prepare himself for the REAL world after high school. Now it is too late. He cannot go back and he struggles to move forward because he is so full of regret now. He told me sadly, "I reminisce all the time." We are working together to build a foundation for his future now. He's got an awesome future and God has given him another chance, but his twenty something transition season is one that is filled with the consequences for failing to listen to wisdom.

## The one thing about the future is that it is always coming.

For many of you, this chapter is no new revelation. You have been grinding yourself into the ground with guilt for months and years because of bad decisions. My advice to you is get up! You can go for so long in this condition that you begin to accept everything that comes to you as something that you deserve. You feel unworthy of God's grace and love. Even when He starts to show light at the end of the tunnel, you turn away from the light and run right back into the mess.

Intentionally, this will be the shortest chapter. I will not dwell on the present because I don't want you to get stuck there either.

We constantly hear about the people who live in the past, but a mindset that holds you in the present without ever considering the future has led you to your current results. In fact, many of you are victims of the "secular" mindset. To be secular means that you live with no view of the eternal, with no consideration of God or spiritual things. It means living totally focused on the here and now without regarding the future. When Jesus said that we should not worry about tomorrow he was speaking concerning worrying about how God was going to take care of us. He was not saying that we live with no plans and no wisdom for tomorrow.

Mass media has methodically indoctrinated millions to believe that embracing the present will lead to happiness. I remember a line from the TV show, Star Trek, in which the captain tells his daughter to seize the moment and to always make the present moment the most important thing in life. Well, many of us have made the present the most important moment and the decisions we have made in those moments have cost us dearly. The one thing about the future is that it is always coming. When it arrives, it becomes your new present moment. When your new moment comes, will you face it with confidence or with regret? Your future is being shaped by your present decisions.

RIGHT NOW before you make another move, just ask yourself, "What do I want for me?" Speak to your own heart. Answer yourself and declare, "I want what God wants for me."

Chapter

# 9

# Repairs
*Broken Places*

# Chapter 9

But whoever listens to me will dwell safely, and **will be secure, without fear of evil.** – (Proverbs 1:33) *

## Insecurity

As a husband and father, I cannot explain the helplessness I feel when I look at the faces of young men and women who have desperately missed the love and affirmation of their parents, in particular, their fathers. Through our years of teaching pre-marital classes and in the spontaneous moments of advice to young people, we have seen the conflict and turmoil that is released in relationships by a thing called **insecurity**. Insecurity will hold you in a vice grip, never allowing you to move successfully to the next level of your life. I see insecurity as one of the most dominant elements to cause young women to doubt or compare themselves to others. If they get married they crave something their husbands just cannot give them. Insecurity has dominated the hearts of young men who lose themselves in indecision and inconsistency. They are frustrated because they just cannot seem to do enough. They do not feel adequate or competent. If they get married, the pain in their wives and children only reinforces the awareness of their inabilities. Whether married or single, men and women try to fill the empty and broken places with work, activities, or even ministry. Insecurity results from the fear of having one's weaknesses exposed. You are never sure if you will be accepted especially if people find out who and what you really are.

When I see the hurt in the eyes of my sons and daughters how I wish I could hold them, like a father, and just take the pain away. There are those who felt and still feel uncomfortable receiving the simple expression of a hug because their lives have

**135**

been filled with perverted motives behind a physical touch. Carol and I have often discussed different teenagers and young adults who took anywhere from one to ten years before they ever allowed us to touch them. When we heard their stories, we understood why. One young lady told me, "Please forgive me for never giving you and your wife a hug; I'm just not used to the father-mother thing." She went on to say that since her father was not in her life, she just wasn't comfortable with expressing affection. It was very hard to look at someone who needed this kind of assurance and affirmation and not be able to do anything about it. We often felt we had to back away because we did not want to invade or violate their conscience. I do not think it is right to embrace or touch someone if they are not comfortable with you. You never move too far or too fast in any relationship. Their insecurity dictates the pace. In an urban, inner city ministry like we have worked in, we have found insecurity to be one of the major, yet underrated issues in the church.

### "Daddy, am I pretty?"

Many felt uncomfortable with us for the simple reason they just did not know us. Once they got to know us, it was still a long process of building up confidence and trust. It takes a long time to build trust. Many young people had been so disappointed by those they trusted that they did not want to give us an opportunity to disappoint them, too. They did not know if they could trust us with their secrets and faults. Would we still love and accept them if we knew what their real pains and struggles were? As a spiritual father, I can hear little boys saying, "Watch this daddy! Am I doing it right?" I can hear little girls still asking, "Daddy, am I pretty?" Even as I write this, the pain in my heart brings tears to my eyes because I am aware of the broken places in them. What many people in their twenty something years are asking is, "Will you love me even after you find out what I am really like?" Due to a family's or church's code of ethics and religious attitudes, thousands have been turned away and rejected when they disclosed their deepest darkest secrets.

They thought they could confide in someone they trusted, but they found their "business" broadcast throughout their family or church community. Rather than finding acceptance, they found self-righteous judges whose only verdict was guilt and condemnation.

## Family Fault Lines

In October of 1999, one of my brothers passed away. Due to the dark secrets surrounding his death, some people in the St. Louis community attended the funeral to see how our family would handle the explanation of his death. As a family involved in the spiritual leadership of our city, we could not dance around the issues and allow insecurity to dictate the future of our family and ministry. God directed me to turn the focus from my brother's faults to our entire family's faults. I was given the opportunity to share a priceless revelation. I read it in the service. Special friends and pastors were there from all over the country. When it was my turn to speak I had no idea the impact the words I shared would have. Here is a portion of that message:

## My Brother's Life (Family Fault Lines)

Home going Celebration of Elder Mark Green,
November 1, 1999

Tuesday morning, October 26, 1999 (two days after Mark's death) I awakened this morning with a song that the Lord had given me back in February of 1998. I found my journal and read the words again:
**In a heartbeat, the prodigal son was brought back into the fold and the elder son was told to love this way. Now we must be radical sons, bring our brothers back into the fold and share the love of Jesus & His grace.**
I did not completely embrace its meaning until now. I must say

that growing up with Mark was fun, fast, and furious. Pam, Jonny, and I were born after Lillian, Ray, Mark, and Irwin. Irwin died while momma was pregnant with me and I came into the world into a grief stricken family. Mark was the one who often communicated life's realities to the three younger siblings. When he told us that he was going to give us a whipping, we would say, 'We are going to tell daddy.' He would say, 'By the time daddy gets home, I will have already finished.' So another one of life's realities was settled. Mark was the first person I ever hit in the face with my fist. The color of his eyes changed and I knew that he was the last person that I would ever hit in the face with my fist. He became the first person to ever get his hands around my neck. Then I discovered how strong my skinny brother was and a new respect for him was introduced into my world.

As the years went by, we became friends. He allowed me to be his college dorm roommate in his final year at Oral Roberts University. Imagine letting your kid brother live with you in your last year of college. He accepted my friend (and future wife) and was the first to welcome her into our family. Mark had a great desire for family and mending broken hearts, but it was because he was living with a broken heart many times himself.

The Bible says that we are to confess our faults one to another that we may be healed. The word fault does not simply mean guilt or wrong doings. A fault is a place of tension, a place where you are fragile, cracked, broken, and pressured to the point where you are about to snap and cause great devastation like the fault lines in the earth's crust that reach points of pressure; that cause earthquakes. Confess your earthquake potential points to one another. Confess your broken places. Confess your fragile places. Confess your pain. My brother, Mark, sometimes did not think he could confess his real pain. I now believe that after the death of his baby brother, he did not want to be a burden to an already devastated family. I see that pattern in all of us now.

Earlier this year after Mark organized a Green family weekend of prayer and fellowship, we had promised to get together for an all brothers night out. I see now that Mark was trying to set up a moment that he could talk about some of our family's pain. If we had had that brother's night out we might have asked each other the questions that needed to be asked about our family. We might have asked what it was like for our mother to have a child out of wedlock in the moral failure forbidding times of 1949. We might have asked what it was like for that child, our older half sister, to feel rejected all of her life. We might have asked Ray, what it was like to live under the scrutiny and expectations to be perfect all the time. We might have asked him, what is was like for our sister-in-law to be a pastor's wife living with a dark secret of abortion all those years before she disclosed it to our congregation. We might have talked about what it was like for our younger sister to live through a divorce while in the spotlight as a worship leader in her big brother's church. We might have asked our younger brother what is was like to be the youngest child overlooked and left behind with hardly anyone around to partake in some of the special moments and events in his life. I could have told them what it was like for me to struggle with spirits of rage, murder, lust, and infirmity in a family full of preachers. We might have asked Mark about his pain, his fragile places, and his point of an earthquake-like disaster. How could we be so close, so anointed, so mightily used of God without knowing each other's pain? In church we all do the same thing. We ask, how are you doing, brother? And we religiously answer, "I am blessed!" But deep inside, we are broken.

My brother was one to worship through his weakness and praise through his pain. There was pain and brokenness that, for many reasons, he must have felt he could not confess. I know that confessing my faults means apologizing for what I did wrong, but it also means revealing who I really am. We all played a part in each other's inability or unwillingness to go all the way with this. However, these thoughts of mine are not an attempt to place blame or seek sympathy. This is merely my

**139**

observation of our family and our lives connected to Mark.

Three years ago we celebrated the home going of our grandmother, Genorah Stewart. Granny left a legacy of prayer and the word. A legacy of music, praise and worship has also been passed on to us. If they can come, it will be nice to see my cousins. We probably won't have much time together after this is over. We will have to grieve quickly, get back to living, and continue to deal with the tremors within us warning of impending, earthquakes. We must find a time and get with our families. We must get below the surface and expose our brokenness and pain. We are all gifted, talented, and anointed. What a family we are, but we are broken and hurting in some areas and relationships. So let's get it right this time.

On Sunday, October 24th, 1999 we finally reached this point as a family. In the previous three weeks we exposed some of our fault lines as a family. God used Mark to bring us to the point of true confession. In those final hours we had moments of reconciliation and repentance with Mark and with each other. A unity came upon us like never before, and as we told Mark we loved him and accepted him regardless of his weakness and fault we lifted up worship to the Lord and Mark left us, going into the presence of the Lord. It was as if that was all he needed to know.

On our first hospital visit (to see Mark), Carol and I walked into the room and I said, "Hello man of God... that is who the Lord told me you are." He broke into tears and I realized that he did not see himself that way. He did not see himself as a preacher, teacher, evangelist or any other title. He simply saw himself as an unworthy worshipper.

Now when I look back over my brother's life and see how God mightily used him in spite of his brokenness, and in spite of his

**140**

pain, I know that it was the grace of God that sustained him. For that is the story of Mark Green, his wife, his children, and his family. Mark Ivory Green was a warrior. Sometimes he was a rebel. He was wounded many times along the way and he bled silently for a lot of years. Most of his years were in obedience to God. Sometimes there was rebellion. But the love of God always drew him back to his purpose and calling. God has been faithful, righteous and just.

## We all have broken places in our lives

Out of that painful experience came a nugget of wisdom about the broken places in our lives. They are like the faults in the earth's crust. From a geological point of view, a fault is a crack created by stress in the earth's crust. I had always thought of a person's fault as just simply being their sins, habits, vices, or behavior. God opened my understanding to see every person's heart and life like the earth, which has stress points that break under pressure. **Where** the break occurs is called a fault. **When** the break occurs it is called an earthquake.

I discovered there are at least three types of stress in the earth's crust. They are **tension, compression and shearing**. The wiles of the enemy are instrumental in triggering our earthquakes. Psalm 51:5 says, "Behold, I was brought forth in iniquity, and in sin my mother conceived me." We were born with the faults. We were born with fissures (splits and cracks in a foundation), which are passed down from generation to generation. It is only a matter of time before the faults erupt under the pressure of sin and the world.

**Tension** pulls a (rock, foundation) person apart forcing opposite sides away from each other. It is the pressure of being torn between right and wrong. This is directly related to sinful behavior and our flesh. Galatians 5:19 says," But when you follow your own wrong inclinations, your lives will produce these

**141**

evil results: impure thoughts, eagerness for lustful pleasure, idolatry, spiritism (that is, encouraging the activity of demons), hatred and fighting, jealousy and anger, constant effort to get the best for yourself, complaints and criticisms, the feeling that everyone else is wrong except those in your own little group — (and there will be wrong doctrine), envy, murder, drunkenness, wild parties, and all that sort of thing."

I believe that Satan targets our fallen fleshy nature and cause tension to literally tear us apart on the inside. Galatians 5:17 says, "For we naturally love to do evil things that are just the opposite from the things that the Holy Spirit tells us to do; and the good things we want to do when the Spirit has his way with us are just the opposite of our natural desires. These two forces within us are constantly fighting each other to win control over us, and our wishes are never free from their pressures." We can know what we are supposed to do, but we have a craving for the forbidden pulling us. When you think of this as tensions in a person's heart, it adjust our view about what a fault is. The tensions will identify the faults, the place in us that is broken. This is the place most likely to cave in under this kind of pressure. That is why sin is not only a behavior, but it is a condition. The quake (behavior) is the manifestation of a deeper issue. The deeper issue is that we were born sinners. We were born fragile and broken. The sinful expression simply indicates that another earthquake has occurred inside of us. You could easily sum up tension in these three ways: Lust of the flesh, Lust of the eye, and the Pride of life (which keeps our lust and pain in darkness & secrecy).

**Compression:** the squeezing of opposites sides against each other. Sometimes the stress on our lives is not necessarily direct enticements to sinful behavior, but it is our response to life itself. Most of us feel squeezed in by at least three categories of life's everyday issues. They are the pressures of:

1.) Daily Responsibility,

2.) Internal Expectations

3.) Societal Morals and Values

## Jobs and bills

The pressures of every day life have literally caused mental and emotional breakdowns in many young adults. Usually at the top of the list is the pressure of going to work everyday and dealing with people. When you hate your job and work it only because you have bills to pay, that leads into more intense compression pressure. The demands of rent, utilities, loans, insurance, food, and clothing has many of you under so much pressure that you cannot sleep. For the Christian, you have the responsibility of tithing and giving to your local church, but see no way you can possibly do that. Yet, when you don't tithe, you don't see any increase. You don't see any increase, so you don't tithe. It is a vicious cycle and the pressure increases until you have another earthquake. This usually results in spending binges and blowing your money on food, clothes, nightclubs, parties, or purchasing expensive things you cannot afford. Some of you have quit jobs and moved from place to place with no financial stability at all. This is an indication of a fault line trembling under the compression of daily responsibilities.

## By the time I am 25, 35, 45....

Often walking hand in hand with daily responsibility pressure is the expectation you have on yourself. Most people live with a mental timeline of where they want to be by the time they reach a certain age. I have encountered too many self-driven young people. The world calls it self-motivated, but when you have your life on a timeline that is contrary to God's timing, you cause yourself untold, needless heartache and pain. In American football there is a particular penalty called unnecessary rough-

**143**

ness. This penalty is usually called when someone throws in an extra punch while tackling someone or if they pull someone down after the official blows the whistle to tell everyone to stop playing. They are penalizing them for over aggressiveness and playing beyond the boundaries and rules of the game. Please allow me to say that God has blown the whistle and called an unnecessary roughness penalty on many of you. You are playing outside of the boundaries and rules of the game. Part of the reason you are playing outside the boundaries is because you think the game clock is going to run out on you. In your mind, you believe thirty or forty is too old to accomplish certain goals. The world's mass media has done a great job in promoting youthfulness. They have taken the honor out of maturity and the things that are worth waiting for. Thousands are in the rat race trying to beat the world's time clock. It is a serious compression that is squeezing you. You see more things that you cannot fit into your lifestyle because of the big squeeze. Usually the first things to go are the principles of God and His Word. Men will sacrifice their wives and babies to beat the clock. Women will sacrifice their husbands and babies to beat the clock. Notice how in both instances the children are sacrificed in our efforts to beat the clock. I am not writing to debate if wives or husbands should stay home to raise the children. Obviously, there are vast numbers of couples that must work outside the home to make ends meet. The issue for this time is to point out the reality that we tend to lose our children while striving against this kind of pressure. Too often we assume that since our parents raised us this way and we have turned out okay, that we can do the same with our own children. Let's take a closer look. **We are not okay.** Part of the brokenness inside of us is due to the absence of our parents during our formative years. It is not long before the internal earthquake erupts and you explode on your friends, family, coworkers, and church leaders because you cannot keep up with the pace anymore.

A very dear woman in our church told us of the time she was raising her children and wanting to advance in her career. She hurriedly tried "potty" training her youngest child so that she could put her into daycare and begin a new job. Years later, she discovered that the child often wet herself in the daycare and was deeply wounded inside when no one helped her. She grew up feeling abandoned and helpless. Insecurity was deeply embedded in her soul. Looking back, this precious woman was filled with regret for being so driven and insensitive to the needs of her child. She thought, like many do today, that her child would be okay. She was not okay and it took years of prayer and counseling to bring healing to her daughter. **The moral of this story- don't be driven, but be given to the will of God**.

## I Don't Think So (Societal Pressure)

Back in the days when we were teen ministry pastors, God gave me a song for a lesson I was teaching to encourage young people to stand up for what they believe. We later dramatized the song in a musical. Some of the lyrics went like this:

GET AN EDUCATION GET AN EDUCATION
GET TO GRADUATION TO GET A DEGREE
GET A GOOD JOB, MAKE A LOT OF MONEY
MAKE A LOT OF MONEY, AND YOU CAN BE FREE
HAVE A LOT OF SEX, HAVE A LOT OF SEX
MAKE A NEW BABY, GET A DISEASE
NATIONAL HEALTH PLAN, GOVERNMENT PROTECTION
MAKE IT PRO-CHOICE, KILL IT WITH EASE
LESBIAN MOTHER, GOOD GAY DAD
MAYBE TWO MOMMY'S, NOTHING IS BAD
CALL IT HOMOPHOBIA, CALL IT COMING OUT
ORIENTATION, TENSIONS MOUNT

TRUE LOVE WAITS, TRUE LOVE WAITS
ABSTINENCE WORKS THERE'S NO DEBATE
TAKE THE GENOCIDE FROM CAPITAL HILL
DO I HEAR HITLER IN THE HEALTH PLAN BILL?
GODLY MOTHERS, PRIESTLY DADS

**145**

BROTHERS GO HOME TO THE KIDS YOU HAD
YES IT'S A PHOBIA, NOT AGAINST THE GAY
IT'S THE WRATH OF GOD THAT'S COMING THIS WAY

WILL I CONFORM TO THE SYSTEM?
AND BE LIKE EVERYBODY ELSE?
BE A ZOMBIE INDIVIDUAL?
LIKE THE ONES WHO NEVER REALLY CARED?
WILL I CHOOSE THE RIGHT TO END A LIFE?
EXCHANGE MY SEXUALITY?
LET SOMEONE ELSE DECIDE MY PATH?
LET SATAN JUST RUN OVER ME?
I DON'T THINK SO
CHRIS GREEN, HEART OF THE NATION MUSIC, 1995

Obviously, this book is not an attempt to speak out on these and many other issues of our times, but it is an opportunity to acknowledge the pressure that Christian young adults are living under all the time. It is very difficult to live and work without facing at least one of the issues in that song. One of our spiritual daughters came home from college after her first year and told us that everything that they portrayed in that musical selection (I Don't Think So) had become things that she faced immediately in college. Day after day, the pressure is constantly on you. The peer pressure of high school does not compare to this kind of pressure. Now your job, a promotion, a scholarship and even your very livelihood can be on the line, (based upon you expressing or remaining silent on the issues in the world today). It is not long before convincing arguments and viewpoints begin to make sense to you. The pressure is great and a compromise here and there eventually leads to the earthquake, and you give in. Maybe not on everything in your faith, but on enough issues to cause you to begin to doubt key scriptures of the Bible. It is not long before you find yourself reasoning that if one or two scriptures are wrong, then maybe Jesus Christ was not always right either. If Jesus Christ was not always right, then maybe He is not the Son of God. If that is true, then maybe this whole thing about God and Christianity is all a bunch of religious foolishness. It is a dangerous path to start down, but the pressures of society are pushing you in this direction constantly. My pastor, Raphael Green, calls this The Lure of the Logical Lie. He taught on this for months and the entire teaching series is recommended to all of our young people who graduate from high school and go on to college. I recommend this teaching series to you also. He has taught that there are many things that make sense, but they are still lies. They are logical lies. There are many things in society that are normal, but they still aren't right. It is abnormal normality. There is a way that seems right, but it ends in death. This is a serious pressure that you live with all the time and the word of God, on these issues, will fortify you so you can stand up to this compression with overcoming grace and strength.

**Shearing:** violent glances of opposite sides against each other in opposing, but parallel directions.So many of us are not only broken because of the tension of the flesh and the compressions of society, but we have been seriously damaged due to violent encounters in life (shearing). The natural results of shearing are that parts and pieces of the opposing sides are torn off. There is damage, defacing, and destruction. Shearing is direct conflict and confrontation. As you are going through the twenty something years, much of the damage of shearing begins to surface in your life. You realize the parts and places that have been sheared. Those who grew up under domination, manipulation, intimidation, abuse (emotional, verbal, physical or sexual), violence, poverty, divorce, desertion or separation are, reluctantly, being forced to see how shearing has affected their outlook on life. This affects their ability and willingness to go through life's transitions.

### The damage of childhood days may just now be surfacing

Carol's parents were separated when she was twelve years old. Ten years later when she married me (a major life transition), her biggest fear was that I would leave her. It was a fear that haunted her all the time. She was afraid of even the slightest conflict or argument between us. It took many years of nurturing before this fear was eased out of her heart.

During this time of your life, deep hurts from past conflicts begin to haunt you. You are already facing many unknown, unfamiliar, and new challenges in your life and just mentioning the past automatically causes some anxiety. However your anxiety is an indicator and an opportunity to open and expose sheared places that you may have buried for years. You may find yourself battling with the memories of a rape, incest, criminal assault, or physical abuse. The shearing affects of divorce, separation, or family feuds are affecting you in ways that you never imagined. Even the damage of early childhood days may just now be surfacing. I was once the butt of jokes in the classroom, schoolyard and even in church. When I was ten years old my "best friends" beckoned me to leave a church service and join them in the boys' restroom. When I entered the restroom, one grabbed me from behind and held my arms behind my back while the other punched me in the chest. The blow did not physically hurt near as much as the blow of betrayal and deception. It was as if a part of me was punched off. It was a moment that I buried emotionally. It caused me to embrace a fear of rejection, which followed me right into my marriage. After this and many other negative experiences, I shut down and stopped talking from the time I was eleven years old until I met my wife to be in college at eighteen. I did not trust anybody who tried to get close to me. I was very cautious and reserved when I met Carol. It took almost a year for me to open up and admit how I felt about her. I did not realize how much that restroom experience affected me until years after we were married and I told Carol this story. I burst into tears and cried like a little boy in her arms. I had no idea how much that childhood event had sheared me.

## Pass the salt, please

Shearing is still very much a part of your life. No doubt, there are confrontations with family, friends, teachers, co-workers, or church leaders that are, right now, having the affect of shearing. When there are glancing blows coming against you, the responses are often as violent as the initial blow. There may be an outward explosion or an inward implosion, but either way, it is the release of the earthquake.

Dr. Lynn Lucas, who pastors the Fountainhead Church in Long Island, New York, shared with our congregation the interesting fact that in areas of the earth where there are high concentrations of salt, there are no devastating earthquakes. This is because, under pressure, salt liquefies and filters into cracks and crevices and holds the broken places together, thus preventing the violent shakings that cause great damage in an earthquake. She told us salt, in the Bible, represents a preserving element as well as a covenant level of commitment. I believe that it is going to involve some covenantal relationships and some preserving steps in your life to get you through the twenty something years. By trying to preserve yourself and staying away from any close relationship, you only run the risk of being isolated and alone with the tremors that are warning you of an impending quake. By getting involved in a church and its home Bible study or fellowship groups, you will establish the kinds of preserving elements and covenant bonding that will help you deal with shearing pressures.

I am definitely no expert so I strongly recommend the book, "No Longer A Victim" co authored by Dr. Lynn Lucas and Burton Stokes. It is great source of guidance and healing for you in this time of your life. This season of your life can be one of healing and repairs instead of perpetual pain and endless hurting. Please don't remain alone and isolated. I know there is great risk in stepping outside the safety zone of your own thoughts, experiences and secrets, but it is worth the risk. Most people exist just to grab temporary and fleeting minutes of pleasure that are followed by years of pain. You can begin to break that cycle. Yes, there will be moments of pain, but you can have a lifetime of healing.

**Think of it like this:** If you severely sprain or break your ankle, there will be tremendous pain as a physician examines you and does whatever is necessary to set it and wrap it. There will be days of pain that follow, but because you are moving in the right direction towards healing, you bear the pain and keeping working with the injured area. Eventually you will see and feel the healing process. I believe it is the same where we have experienced emotional, mental, and spiritual injuries.

Coming out of that painful time in the fall of 1999, I wrote the following song. I pray that it directs you toward the healing you may need for the injuries you have suffered in your life.

## Fault Lines

In my family I see a constant pressure.
There's a field of wheat and tares growing up together.
I go to church; I'm told the positive always express.
But the Bible says the fault in me is what I must confess.

I got a treasure in this earthen vessel,
But the vessel's weak. I've got a broken handle.
If anybody knew what I carried inside
Could they ever see past my fault lines?

So much shearing and tearing, compression
Deep underground, there's so much pressure
Devastation, when we break inside
We can no longer hide our secret fault lines

**150**

We are cracked and broken; no more we can take
Foundations crumble in a terrible quake
So yield your secret, surrender the pride
Jesus heals and fills secret fault lines

Chris Green, Heart of the Nation Music, 2000

# What's For Dinner?

*Give Me the Recipe*

## Chapter 10

Don't you love walking into a home and being greeted by the wonderful aromas of a meal being prepared? You find yourself asking, "What's for dinner?" because the smell is so inviting. Simmering pots and pans with steam filling the kitchen have caused my mouth to water in anticipation. Sometimes even the sound of frying fish or chicken can cause my stomach to rumble. That is what this book has attempted to do. Hopefully, the smell of success in the will of God has made you ask, "What's for dinner?" I have tried to stir your appetite. Perhaps you have tasted a little bit of the potential for your life and you want to know what the ingredients are in the sauce. Many good meals have made people ask for the recipe.

Maybe I have sparked a few questions. You may have wished I expounded more and given details (I wish I could have done so, too). I am sure there are areas where you needed me to go deeper. If this has happened, then I have fulfilled my goals for this book. At least you are open to getting more understanding and answers. You are at the point where you are asking the very title of this book: **What now?** Well, now is the time for you to get connected with those who can go deeper and give more details. Find the people who will love you and be committed to you. Once you find them, you must make a commitment to stick with them. The desire I have is for you to get help and find the path God has for your life. I have discussed a lot with a few words. The idea has been to give you an opportunity to evaluate where you are with God, others, and yourself.

The best place to look for the deeper connection is the local church. There is a wealth of resources there. You will find your spiritual parents. You will learn how to work out relationships. You will get prepared for your life. You can learn how to develop intimacy with God. You can start getting answers to life's tough questions. You can get healed. If you are not in one, find a church where the pastors and leaders are genuine. Find a church where you can honestly say, "In this house, I know I can grow in grace and the knowledge of Jesus Christ." No church is perfect because people are not perfect, but you must find a place where you can be planted like a seed. You will need to let your roots go deep to experience strength and stability.

There is a short list of helpful resources at the end of this book. My role has been to point you to them and others who can help you. In many ways I am not qualified to go into the details and deep places, but they are.

I am convinced you are part of a generation destined for greatness, but greatness comes out of adversity and trial. Obviously, I do not know what the future holds. Some predict prosperity and the good times rolling in. Others are crying in the street warning of devastation all over the world. I believe we will see both happening and the nuggets of wisdom offered in these pages will prepare your heart and soul to take on the outcomes of the good, the bad, and the ugly. God is not so overly conscious of the whole world that He is not mindful of you and your world. At the same time, He is not so wrapped up in your world that He cannot see the bigger picture of the whole world. This wisdom will keep you in balance. It will keep you locked in with the will of God for your life even when your world and the whole world seem to be falling apart.

## Join with me in prayer.

### Father God,

I pray, in the name and authority of Jesus Christ, for every person who picked up this book. I pray this especially for those who are in their transitional twenties. They read it because this transition is more difficult than they could ever have imagined. They feel like your disciples who were caught in a storm on the sea. They are being battered by the winds and waves. It is the most frightening thing in the world to see they are about to be killed trying to make this crossing in life. They cannot go back to the way things used to be, yet they do not know if they can make it to the other side, either. This is a difficult transition. Even You Lord, seem to be far away.

Someone, who read this book, has no particular religious background. Though many things I wrote, made sense, still others issues are more like fantasy. I ask you to open the eyes and understanding of everyone who took the time to read this book. They read it because they need answers. They read it because they want a hope and a future. They know there is something better than where they have been. They want to believe there is something better than where they are now. So I ask You to impart into each heart, right now, a new ability to grasp these nuggets of wisdom for their lives. Give grace to those who are suffering great anguish from bad decisions. Give grace to those who are broken by the earthquakes of life. Give grace to the fatherless, the motherless, and the friendless.

I thank You for making crooked paths straight, for filling in the valleys, and bringing low, the mountains. I thank You for the preparation that has been made in every heart and home so Jesus Christ and the wonderful purpose and plan He has, will be fulfilled completely. I thank You for opening up each life so each one has the potential to have this testimony spoken of it: "They fulfilled the purpose of God in their generation."

And now, by Your authority, I call each one out of darkness and into the light. May each one see You and see himself or herself in a brand new way from this day forward. In the name, nature, and authority of Jesus Christ, I humbly submit this prayer to you Father God. Amen (Let it be so)

Though this is the conclusion of this book I prophetically pronounce, it is a new beginning in your life.

# Bibliography

1, * The Holy Bible, New King James Version, (Nashville, Tennessee: Thomas Nelson, Inc.) 1982.
2-5 W.E. Vine, Merrill F. Unger and William White, Vine's complete expository dictionary of Old and New Testament words [computer file], electronic ed., Logos Library System, (Nashville: Thomas Nelson) 1997, c1996.

**From Chapter 1-** "God is supposed to supply all my need" taken from Bible reference:
"And my God shall supply all your need according to His
riches in glory by Christ Jesus." Philippians 4:19

**From Chapter 4-** "head and not the tail" and "above and not beneath" taken from Bible reference: "And the LORD will make you the head and not the tail; you shall be above only, and not be beneath," Deuteronomy 28:13

**From Chapter 4-** "more than a conqueror" taken from Bible reference "Nay, in all these things we are more than conquerors through him that loved us" Romans 8:37

**Chapter 5** is based on teaching from Pastor Raphael Green: "Getting Started" Discipleship Manual. Metro Christian Worship Center

**Chapter 6-** "breakthrough conferences, workshops and seminars" is not a reference to or critique of any particular conference, workshop or seminar that carries the name Breakthrough in its description, intents, themes, purpose, or mission statement.

**Chapter 6-** "We are conquerors! No, we are more than conquerors! We are over comers!" taken from Bible reference "Nay, in all these things we are more than conquerors through him that loved us" Romans 8:37

**From Chapter 7-** "If you love me, you will obey my commands." taken from Bible reference: "If you love Me, keep My commandments." John 14:15

**Chapter 8-** "When Jesus said that we should not worry about tomorrow…" taken from Bible reference "Therefore do not worry about tomorrow, for tomorrow will worry about its own things. Sufficient for the day is its own trouble." Matthew 6:34

**Chapter 9-** All geological information provided by the Compton's Interactive CD Encyclopedia, 1999 Edition

# Suggested Resources

Recognizing the Voice and Will of God-
Real Faith-
The Lure of the Logical Lie-
My Pain Does Not Stop- Raphael Green
(Audio teaching series)

> Metro Christian Worship Center
> 3452 Potomac
> St. Louis, MO. 63118
> 314-772-8444
> www.metrocwc.org, email: tapes@metrocwc.org

No Longer A Victim – Burton Stokes and Lynn Lucas –
> Fountain Head Congregation Church
> PO Box 431
> East Northport, NY 11731-0431

Understanding Your Potential –
Releasing Your Potential –
The Pursuit of Purpose – Dr. Myles Munroe – Bahamas Faith
Ministries

Sex and Dating – Dave Burrows – Bahamas Faith Ministries
> The Diplomat Center
> Carmicheal Rd.
> P.O. Box N-9583, Nassau, Bahamas
> www.bfmmm.com

Sex and the Bible -
Sex Is A Spiritual Act - Dr. Dale Conaway –
> Purity Press Publishers
> P.O. Box 2896
> Decatur, GA 30031

Will The Real Enemy Please Stand Up?
Stop The Hurting, Lord
Fatal Attractions of the Christian Kind
Bone of My Bone- Dr. Clarence and Ja'ola Walker
(Audio Cassette Teaching Series)
        Clarence Walker Ministries
        P.O. Box 15522
        Philadelphia, Pennsylvania 19131
        www.cwministries.org


Christopher and Carol Green - Fruitful Life Productions

Music CD's:
Our Story, His Songs (Celebrating our marriage and life)
It's A Family Thing  (Special family moments)
Remnant Catcher Revue
Generations and Praise "A Personal Touch"

Our Most Requested Messages: (Cassette or CD)
Fruitful Lives

Carol Green:
What Are We Reproducing?
For the Joy Set Before Us
Reconciled With The Past, Ready For The Future

Chris Green:
Let's Go Shopping
In it to Win It
No Longer Denied, But Identified (A 21st Century Man)
Living Letters (Never Judge A Book By Its Cover)

Contact us for information or engagements at
        Metro Associates, Inc.
        3501 Arkansas
        St. Louis, MO 63118
        314-772-8993
        www.Fruitful-Life.net

# About the author

Christopher Green has served as the senior associate pastor of Metro Christian Worship Center of St. Louis, Mo. founded by Raphael & Brenda Green, since 1987. Chris and his wife Carol also support the senior pastor as Teen and Single Adults ministry's Oversight Pastors. Chris has also overseen the Radio and TV, the audio/ video/ computer multi-media departments and the business management of the local church.

Officially ordained as pastors in May 1992, after extensive Biblical & practical training, Chris & Carol introduced a very unique style and approach to teen ministry. Taking the themes and lessons of wisdom from the book of Proverbs, they ministered to teens from a father's instruction and a mother's teaching point of view. They used cultural and ethnic expressions of music, rap and dance in the weekly teen meetings to help young people identify with the move of God in their generation. They have written over 70 songs that have been used in praise and worship for children, teens, and the local church's community outreach effort.

Next they were assigned oversight to the College & Career Ministry, where they provided wisdom and insight for the challenges of the 21st century young adult. The one major difference in their approach to this ministry was the inclusion of both married and single young adults. They started this ministry by focusing on the issues common to all young adults regardless of marital status. This opened up into a dynamic Internet web forum called the Remnant Catcher Network and has also initiated an innovative outreach called Remnant Catcher. The RC format of comedy, music, drama, poetry, and worship led to a ground swell of excitement and participation. This ministry eventually led to the establishment of a thriving singles ministry called G.I.F.T.S. (God's Internally Fortified and Tested Singles).

Chris and Carol raised youth ministry leaders in their home church and answered the call to speak in local, national and international youth conferences. Their focus has been the post high school young adult. Chris serves on the board of the International Youth Leaders Association based in Nassau, Bahamas under the leadership of Pastor Dave Burrows (Youth Pastor of Bahamas Faith Ministries, Dr. Myles Munroe).

Chris also serves as vice president of Metro Associates, Inc., which is a community outreach ministry in the south St. Louis area. From this position, since 1989,he has helped coordinate annual street music concerts and events. He has produced an award winning cable TV broadcast called Urban Liberation and established two music production companies called Heart of the Nation Music and Metro Arts Publishing, through the Arts & Productions division of Metro Associates. He's produced music CD's and tapes for children, teens and families.

Chris & Carol have been married since December 1980 and are the proud parents of three sons: Christopher, Jonathan, and David as well as a host of spiritual sons and daughters throughout the world.

## Endorsments

"The only thing worse than being lost, is having no resources to help you find your way. The book **"What Now"** is that much needed road map for anyone lost in transition during this journey called life. Pastor Chris Green's willingness to be brutally honest about his journey through the twenty-something season makes the reader feel that they are not alone, nor the only one feeling confused, frustrated, and overwhelmed. Young people are simply looking for something real, something honest. Pastor Chris' stories hit home in a simple yet profound way. His words come straight from his heart, getting to the heart of the matter. Certainly anointed to touch the hearts of adults, young and old alike."

**- Dr. Debbye Turner,**
  **Miss America 1990, Motivational Speaker, TV Broadcaster**

"The road to destiny is often filled with pain and uncertainty...
**"What Now"** provides an excellent spiritual road map to help you navigate through the pain of your past into the purpose of your today".

**- Dr. Dale H. Conaway, Author/Lecturer**
  **CEO, Purity Press Publishers**
  **President Sword Of The Spirit Ministries, Lithonia, GA.**

I felt I was reading portions of the story of my life in **"What Now"**. The problem was, many times I didn't have answers for the problems I encountered through my turbulent teens and early twenties. This book addresses relevant issues that every young person is currently, or will face. It not only addresses the issues and questions of life, but it also provides sound, biblical, practical answers. Every concerned parent and youth leader

should read this book and place a copy into the hands of youth struggling with life's issues.
- **Pastor Mark Lawrence**
  **Executive Pastor Calvary Revival Church**
  **Norfolk, Virginia, USA**

This is a phenomenal and timely book! The personal examples and willingness to be transparent bring an added dimension, which allows the reader to identify, relate, learn and grow.
I'm convinced that this is not just another book, but an assignment given by God that will be a needed resource and textbook for generations to come. I certainly wish I had something like this when I was in my twenties. We will certainly use this book in our church, as a guideline and workbook for our young adult group.

I highly recommend this book to Pastors and Young Adult Group leaders as a resource and textbook, it will bring understanding and wisdom in discovering God's purpose for all, particularly the twenty-something generation.
- **Frank King, Senior Pastor**
  **Refreshing Waters Worship Center – Kansas City, Mo**

In this book Chris has addressed an area that has often been overlooked in the body of Christ. We have programs and plans for youth and we have programs and plans for adults. There are some who are in somewhat of a no man's land whose needs are not being adequately addressed. In this book, Chris fills the gap in a way that leaves little left to be said.
- **Pastor Dave Burrows**

"Chris Green is a passionate man addressing our greatest treasure, our youth"
- **Dr. Donald Hilliard, 2nd Baptist Church, Perth Amboy, NJ**